DISCIPLES
IN
DIFFICULT DAYS

DISCIPLES
— IN —
DIFFICULT DAYS
Standing Firm in the Faith

ZOE M. SIMPSON

 Lifeline Publishing

St. Catherine, Jamaica W.I.

Published by Lifeline Publishing
St. Catherine, Jamaica
lifeline.2023@yahoo.com
Telephone: (876) 366-8226

The introductory anecdotes, which are the lived experiences of real people, are used with permission. The names of the individuals have been changed.

Cover Concept: Lifeline Designs
Cover Design: Olivia Designs

Author contact: The author may be contacted at zoem.simpson@hotmail.com

To my grandchildren:
Eden, Judah, Jace, Liam,
and their peers who will come to faith
and will need to know how to posture
during the difficult days that will become
their lived experiences.

"Stand firm in the Lord in this way, dear friends!"

—Philippians 4:1

Preface

I t would be presumptuous of me to think that I could ever walk beside the prophet Ezra about whom it was said, "For Ezra had devoted himself to the study and observance of the Law of the LORD, and to teaching its decrees and laws in Israel" (Ezra 7:10). I readily confess that I have not always lived the Word; this remains a constant struggle and a matter about which I earnestly ask the Holy Spirit for help. However, there is nothing that gives me more joy than studying and sharing the Word of God.

I felt a 'call' to Christian ministry while I was in high school. However, I pursued a career in education immediately after graduation. Teaching was fulfilling, but the pull toward Christian ministry resided in my spirit and eventually led me to pursue studies in theology. Although I have not assumed pastoral ministries following my theological studies, I live with a sense of commitment to study and share the word of God.

I was privileged to share the Word of God on the "Grace Hour" radio programme of the Missionary Church Association in Jamaica from 2002 to 2013, while I served the denomination as Christian Education Director. The scriptural reflections in this book are part of a series of presentations that I shared on the radio programme during the period. Granted, the presentations have been somewhat modified.

I am acutely aware that the day will come when I will be unable to teach the Word of God. It is with this awareness that I have "packaged" the presentations in this book. It is my sincere hope that believers in Christ Jesus may find strength for their souls and remain steadfast and true to the faith as they navigate difficult days.

Contents

Introduction

I had purposefully sat with my two sons to watch the movie that re-enacted the crucifixion of Jesus. At the end of the movie, I seized the moment to ask the boys whether they would also want to follow Jesus. With childlike honesty, the elder boy emphatically replied: "Oh no, mummy; I do not want them to beat me up like how they beat up Jesus."

The five-year-old boy's innocent response aptly reflects the awareness that Christ Jesus endured difficult days as He traversed the corridors of earth to fulfil His ministry of reconciling mankind with God. Likewise, those who pledge allegiance to Him will have difficult experiences.

The difficult days of Jesus' sojourn culminated with Him being crucified. This form of punishment is believed to be among the worst, most excruciating, and humiliating forms of punishment in His day. Yet, Jesus endured the suffering and shame of the cross (Hebrews 12:2). Before leaving the earth, Jesus was careful to inform His disciples that they, too, would experience difficult days. "I have told you these things, so that in me you may have peace. In this world you will have trouble. But take heart! I have overcome the world" (John 16:33).

It is, therefore, erroneous to think that coming to faith in Jesus Christ excludes the believer from trials and suffering. Nothing is farthest from the truth! "In fact, everyone who wants to live a godly life in Christ Jesus will be persecuted ..." (2 Timothy 3:12). Those who are followers of Jesus will experience difficulties primarily because the enemy of the Christian faith will spare no means to get believers to recant and retreat and thereby prevent the promulgation of the Gospel of salvation.

In addition to the faith-associated difficulties that believers will inevitably experience, the reality is that believers also live in a real world, with real problems from which they are not exempt. These real-life experiences can also serve to test the faith of believers. Those who are not sufficiently anchored in the knowledge of who God is and in what He says are at risk of caving in. On the other hand, those who know their God and have armed themselves with the mind of suffering (1 Peter 4:1) will be well-equipped to stand firm in the faith during these challenging times.

Scripture has unequivocally stated that "... there will be terrible times in the last days" (2 Timothy 3:1). The "terrible times" will undoubtedly have a negative impact on everyone.

Although there are contending views about the period that is defined as "the last days", Scripture has repeatedly admonished believers in Jesus Christ to "Put on the full armor of God, so that you can take your stand against the devil's schemes." (Ephesians 6:11). While the believers accept and treasure Jesus' invitation to become His disciples and to then make fellow disciples, they must be prepared for the difficult days that will become their reality. The difficulties that believers experience will vary in nature, come from different sources, and have varying intensities and durations.

Believers should take a cue from the Novel Coronavirus (COVID-19) pandemic, which descended upon the world unannounced at the end of 2019 and claimed, in its wake, the lives of countless individuals. History informs us of the realities of previous pandemics. However, since we were not experientially privy to any of those antecedents, to us, the COVID-19 experience was incomparable.

We reflect on the early days of the pandemic and acknowledge that it significantly altered the way we lived and conducted business. The most significant alteration was the physical distancing of individuals that was imposed as a means of containing the spread of the virus. This imposition limited the extent to which we socially interacted with each other. Innately, we are social beings. We thrive on social exchanges. It was, therefore, challenging to come to terms with the new order of isolation, quarantine, and lockdowns.

The pandemic also had a deleterious effect on our mental health. Fear and anxiety were the order of the day in the face of the reality that we were all fighting an invisible enemy, and it was claiming the lives of many.

However, the pandemic experience was not altogether negative. We were forced to devise and implement creative measures to survive. Technology bridged the divide and provided us with the means to connect remotely. Within the Christian community, the church quickly adopted mechanisms that facilitated remote gatherings. The experience prompted some of us to re-examine the Scriptures and our interpretations of several passages. It also deepened our appreciation for the Scriptures pertinent to the unfolding of history and world events.

As the medical experts presented the world with a vaccine that they perceived was an impressive response to the virus, questions of veracity and validity emerged, occupied our minds, and became a ubiquitous topic of interest. A primary moot that emerged and was fiercely debated surrounded whether to take the vaccine. Within the community of believers in the Christian faith, opinions were wide and varied and equally divisive.

Regardless of how believers responded to the pandemic, the experience served as a poignant reminder and a stark indicator that difficult days have always been and will continue to be a persistent challenge for the Christian community. In this context, believers in Christ Jesus are encouraged to adequately position themselves to face the difficult days that will characterize the present age.

Failure to come to terms with the fact that believers will encounter difficulties often leaves some believers feeling sorry for themselves, causing them to depart from the faith or live in despair. On the other hand, an understanding and acceptance of the fact that followers of Christ Jesus will encounter difficulties helps us to navigate our difficult days successfully. The posture that believers in the past assumed and the principles that they practised during their difficult days enabled them to stand firm in the faith. Their examples have become models of reference for believers of this present age and future ages.

The scriptural reflections in this book examine the lived experiences of believers from past ages and respond to the questions: What lessons may we learn from believers who themselves experienced difficult days? What posture should followers of Jesus assume as they experience difficult days? What are the principles that should guide believers as they encounter difficult days? What are the sources of help that believers have at their disposal as they encounter difficult days? Essentially, the scriptural reflections in this book aim to encourage believers to persevere and maintain their faith as they navigate the challenging days of this present age and the future ages.

PART I
Lived Experiences

1.

Difficult Days of Austerity

Habakkuk 1:1-13; Habakkuk 2, 3

T he committee members gathered for the meeting at the end of what everyone described as having been a busy first day of the week. Various members expressed having had a tedious day. The member who said the opening prayer asked God for the "umph" that we all needed to go through the meeting.

The prayer ended, but one member particularly took umbrage at the use of the word "umph" in communicating with God, who was to be reverenced. She, in fact, made the point that no way would the person have used the word "umph" were she talking with the Governor General. I only wondered whether God had a problem with the use of the word "umph", and whether one can truly have a regular conversation with God, especially during difficult situations.

The book of Habakkuk brings into focus how one believer engaged God in conversations of the heart as he experienced difficult days of economic austerity and lack of supplies. In this context, there are three matters for consideration: the first being the prophet's cries for divine intervention.

Cries for Divine Intervention

The prophet Habakkuk lived in an era when the nation of Judah was overcome by its own sinfulness, which manifested in violence and injustice. In his disgust, God had used the Chaldeans, a neighbouring nation, to inflict punishment on the Judeans. The tone of the book reveals an agony of spirit at the evil which followed from the rule of an unjust and immoral power. The prophet Habakkuk took issue with God's course of action and boldly engaged God in an unrestrained conversation.

> "How long, Lord, must I call for help, but you do not listen? Or cry out to you, "Violence!" but you do not save? Why do you make me look at injustice? Why do you tolerate wrongdoing? Destruction and violence are before me; there is strife, and conflict abounds. Therefore, the law is

paralyzed and justice never prevails. The wicked hem in the righteous, so that justice is perverted" (Habakkuk 1:2-4).

At face value, one might think it contemptuous of Habakkuk to have even questioned God, let alone in the tone in which his questions were delivered. But God was not put off by Habakkuk's questions. He did not think it officious of Habakkuk, a mere mortal, to dare to question the Almighty God.

In fact, God was up to the conversation with Habakkuk to the extent that God supplied, with unmistakable ease, fitting answers to Habakkuk's bold questions. To the first question, God informed Habakkuk that His plan was to punish the nation of Judah, and the Babylonians (also known as Chaldeans) would be His instrument (Habakkuk 1:6-11).

The conversational atmosphere remained inviting and facilitating, and Habakkuk continued his conversation with God with a second question. "Why … do you tolerate the treacherous? Why are you silent while the wicked swallow up those more righteous than themselves?" (Habakkuk 1:13). God continued to be at ease with Habakkuk and again supplied an answer to the troubling question when He said, "For the revelation awaits an appointed time; it speaks of the end and will not prove false. Though it linger, wait for it, it will certainly come and will not delay" (Habakkuk 2:3).

The tone of Habakkuk's questions suggests that he was troubled by the prevailing circumstances, and who better to talk to about the matter than the God who knows all things; the God who has answers for every situation. The indication is that Habakkuk's relationship with God facilitated conversations in which he could unburden his soul. Of course, the Sovereign Lord was not about to take counsel from Habakkuk. He was executing His plan according to His purpose. Yet He took the time to converse with the man who dared to engage Him in a conversation.

Constant Trust in God

The second point for consideration is the consistent and unwavering trust that the prophet demonstrated in God, despite the difficult circumstances. In Chapter 3:17-19, Habakkuk wrote,

> Though the fig tree does not bud and there are no grapes on the vines, though the olive crop fails and the fields produce no food, though there are no sheep in the pen and no cattle in the stalls, yet I will rejoice in the Lord, I will be joyful in God my Savior. The Sovereign Lord is my strength; he makes my

feet like the feet of a deer, he enables me to
tread on the heights.

The response that Habakkuk received from God did not
remediate the presenting socio-economic realities. The things
which supported life and living remained undesirable. The
conditions remained the same in the fields and the herds'
pen. Nothing had changed. The only thing that changed was
Habakkuk's posture and perception of his reality. In place of
the prolonged conversations with God, Habakkuk humbly
accepted God's response and chose to continue trusting
Him.

The command of will that Habakkuk demonstrated is
admirable. He did not allow his mind or his spirit to be
inordinately carried away by the difficult circumstances. He
did not allow his emotions to be influenced by the prevailing
situation. Habakkuk took control of his response to the
situation and willed himself to continue to rejoice in his God.

Confidence in God

The third matter for consideration is the confidence that the
prophet demonstrated in God. According to Wycliffe Bible
Commentary (n.d., p. 675): "The words of men in moments
of crisis often indicate their real and inmost convictions."
Listen to the words of the prophet in Chapter 3:19: "The

Sovereign Lord is my strength; he makes my feet like the feet of a deer, he enables me to tread on the heights."

Hear the depth of confidence that Habakkuk had in God's ability to help him prevail over difficult situations. See the personal faith that he continued to demonstrate in God to provide practical answers to the challenging situations that life dealt him. It was evident that Habakkuk had an unshakeable relationship with God. Little wonder, therefore, that he was able to thrust the presenting issues to the back of his mind and will himself to rejoice in his God.

Positioning to Stand Firm

How do you respond to harsh economic realities? Some individuals turn to gaming and betting in search of an elusive dream. Others look expectantly to politicians and the promises they give for a better tomorrow through programmes and projects. All too often, the places to which we look for answers and the people on whom we depend for solutions fail us.

Like Habakkuk, it is helpful to assume a posture of confidence in the faithfulness of the Sovereign Lord in the midst of economic decline and social unrest. There will not always be plenty on your table. But the God of endless resources is mindful of your situation. Ask Him to provide whatever you may need and believe that He will. If what you have asked for is not forthcoming, still trust in God and make do with what you have.

In the face of lack, and until your situation changes, make the personal decision to rejoice and to be thankful for even the little that you have. Determine that you will not allow your difficult situation to get the better of you. Simply command your spirit to trust the Sovereign God and rejoice.

In my opinion, God does not have an issue with His children asking Him questions. After all, He invites conversations. If you are troubled by a difficult matter, talk to God about it. He is not obliged to answer you in the timeframe or manner that you expect Him to. However, trust His wisdom and His commitment to respond in ways that are good and best.

Dismiss the notion that God is in the far distance, or is busy taking inventory of fallen sparrows, as one man facetiously said. God is near enough to hear your prayer; talk with Him. Know, as well, that God speaks through His written Word. Cultivate the practice of reading the Word of God as recorded in the Holy Bible and be content with what God says and what He does during your difficult days of austerity.

2.

Difficult Days of Adversity

Job 1:1-22

If ever there were a believer in God who experienced difficult days, it was Job. The text that frames the reflections in this chapter, Job 1:1-22, turns the spotlight on Job as he navigated difficult days of adversity in which he suffered loss of enormous proportions.

It is worth repeating that faith in God does not exempt the believer from experiencing difficult days. This fact is ably represented in Job's lived experience. He is introduced in Job 1:1-2 as being a man of spiritual integrity: "In the land of Uz there lived a man whose name was Job. This man was blameless and upright; he feared God and shunned evil."

There is very little to be gleaned about the land of Uz from biblical literature. However, the description given of Job's spiritual standing seems to juxtapose his uprightness against possible evil practices of the day. Outside of the details, it seems sufficient to note that Job's spiritual integrity stood out among that of his contemporaries.

Job was also a man of high morality, a trait that was evident in his response to his children's lifestyle. As Job 1:4-5 informs,

> His sons would hold feasts in their homes, inviting their sisters to join them. After each feast, Job would offer burnt offerings for them, concerned that they might have sinned and cursed God in their hearts. This was his regular practice.

Such was the man who suffered difficult days of adversity, resulting in the loss of his wealth and his children in quick succession.

Loss of Wealth

The extent of the loss of wealth that Job suffered is best appreciated against an awareness of the extent of wealth that he enjoyed. According to Job 1:3-4, "He had seven sons and three daughters. Job was incredibly wealthy, possessing 7,000 sheep, 3,000 camels, 500 yoke of oxen, 500 donkeys, and a large number of servants. He was the wealthiest man in the East."

In Job's day, the indicators of wealth and worth were the number of cattle and sheep that one owned, as well as the number of servants and sons that one had. By all indications, Job was a wealthy man, and his wealth earned him a place of much respect among his contemporaries.

The wealth that Job amassed over time was lost in a very short time. According to Job 1:10-11, Satan approached God, saying,

> Have you not put a hedge around him and his household and everything he has? You have blessed the work of his hands, so that his flocks and herds are spread throughout the land. But now stretch out your hand and strike everything he has, and he will surely curse you to your face.

With God's permission, Satan struck Job so that, in quick succession, he experienced financial loss of magnanimous proportions. The Sabaeans stole his oxen and donkeys and killed his servants. Fire destroyed his sheep and the shepherds at the same time. The Chaldeans stole his camels and killed his remaining servants (Job 1:14-17).

With the loss of livestock and servants, Job's net worth was significantly diminished. This was nothing short of adversity! Yet, "… it appeared that he kept his temper, and bravely maintained the possession and repose of his own soul, in the midst of all these provocations" (Matthew Henry Bible Commentary, n.d., para. 30).

The Loss of His Children

As if losing all his wealth was not enough, Job, soon thereafter, lost all his children during a natural disaster.

> While he was still speaking, yet another messenger came and said, "Your sons and daughters were feasting and drinking wine at the oldest brother's house, when suddenly a mighty wind swept in from the desert and struck the four corners of the house. It collapsed on them, and they are dead, and I am the only one who has escaped to tell you!" (Job 1:18, 19)

Job's children were his joy and crown. He had cared for them like a good father should. He had watched over their moral and spiritual formation like a good father should. Job's children had grown to find their places in the scheme of things and were, apparently, socially and financially in good standing. To have his children all killed at once was more than Job could bear. With the news of their passing, "… Job got up and tore his robe and shaved his head" (Job 1:20).

The shaving of the head and the tearing of the robe were signs that, emotionally, Job was deeply affected by the magnitude of his loss and was in grief of soul and spirit. That was a natural response to the extent of grief that he experienced. "He conducted himself like a man under his afflictions, not stupid and senseless, like a stock or stone, not unnatural and unaffected at the death of his children and servants" (Matthew Henry, n.d., para. 30).

The extent of the loss that Job suffered, both financially and socially, was enough to leave him in a state of emotional imbalance. It was enough to tilt his spiritual stance and make him question the goodness of the God he had consistently feared and served. Figuratively, Job had financially and emotionally "fallen on his face" because of the losses. However, he remained spiritually upright and worshipped the God through whom he had acquired his wealth and his children. Having outwardly expressed his grief, this righteous, spiritually mature man did what he customarily did: he fell to the ground and worshipped his God.

The Posture of Worship

The picture of worship is painted in Job 1:21. Having visibly expressed his grief, "... he fell to the ground in worship and said: 'Naked came I from my mother's womb, and naked I will depart. The Lord gave and the Lord has taken away; may the name of the Lord be praised." Job's words in the face of his adversity indicated that, (1) he was completely submitted to the will of the God that he served; (2) he accepted the fact that all that he had come from the all-sufficient God; (3) his faith in God was not predicated on his prosperity. As Heavenor (1970) said, "The loss of possessions had not entailed the loss of faith. Grief might change his appearance, but it could not cheat him of the consolations of faith" (p. 424).

The posture of worship that Job assumed against the backdrop of his adversity was an indication of his recognition that, although all had changed around him, nothing had changed about the God above him. He had lost all his possessions, but he had not lost sight of his position in God. Job fully recognized that God was God, irrespective of what happened to and around him, and He was still worthy of praise and adoration.

Positioning to Stand Firm

Have you, like Job, suffered adversity and loss of any kind? Loss may take various forms:

- loss of health
- loss of a child through death or rebellion
- loss of a spouse through death or divorce

- loss of friends and status
- loss of a job and finances
- loss of support from family and friends
- loss of property and material possessions

What is your posture in the face of adversity and loss? Would you still worship God in the face of adversity and loss? Worship is the act of admitting that God is mighty and marvellous in every way. It is the unbridled adoration of the might and majesty of God. It is complete acceptance of, and submission to, the will of God. Piper (2016) is of the view that true worship is a display of the worth of God in action and attitude. "True worship is based on a right understanding of God's nature, and it is a right valuing of God's worth" (Piper, 2016, para 19).

Whether you assume a posture of worship in the face of adversity will depend on the correctness of your belief about God. The question, then, is whether your belief about God is correct. The individual who believes that God is great, good, and gracious in all that He does, will be more likely to worship Him even in the face of adversity.

The Sovereign God is worthy of our praise and worship despite our circumstances. We do well, therefore, to look past our positions and possessions, see God for who He is, and assume a posture of worship, even in the face of adversity and loss.

3.

Difficult Days of Loneliness

Job 2:7-10; 29:1-20; 30:20; 42:1-6

Human beings are relational in nature. We naturally desire the presence of other human beings—be it physical or psycho-emotional presence—at one time or the other. It is helpful to know that there are others who will celebrate with us on joyous occasions or weep with us in times of sorrow. The absence of human presence has the tendency to result in feelings of loneliness.

The Surgeon General of the United States of America advises that "loneliness is far more than just a bad feeling—it harms both individual and societal health. It is associated with a greater risk of cardiovascular disease, dementia, stroke, depression, anxiety, and premature death" (Murthy, 2023, p. 4). The emotional state of loneliness is examined in this chapter, which is situated in the book of Job. There are four matters to be considered, the first being the depth of loneliness.

The Depth of Loneliness

The book of Job, Chapter 1:1-22, recounts the difficult days of adversity and loss that Job experienced. He lost his children and all his assets to natural disasters. But Job still had his wife and his friends; at least until they, too, seemed to have left him in the difficult place of isolation and loneliness when his adversity continued with the loss of his health.

According to Job 2:7-8, "… Satan went out from the presence of the Lord and afflicted Job with painful sores from the soles of his feet to the top of his head. Then Job took a piece of broken pottery and scraped himself with it as he sat among the ashes." With the loss of his health, Job was at his lowest. Life could not have been more difficult for him!

Job may have naturally looked to his closest companion, his wife, for care and comfort. How disappointed he must have been when she said: "Are you still maintaining your integrity? Curse God and die!" (Job 2:9). Job's response to his wife betrayed the relational and spiritual distance that her advice seemed to have put between them. Her words sounded to Job like the words of the foolish women of the day (Job 2:10), and not the words of the godly woman that he knew.

The advice that Job's wife gave him may be understood in the context of the negative impact that Job's adversities had on her. His losses were, equally, her losses. To have lost 10 children at once would have left any mother in a state of disequilibrium. This woman must have spoken from a place of emotional brokenness. There is much that could be said about Job's wife in this context. However, the focus will be kept on how Job maintained his spiritual integrity by dismissing the ill-advice that he received from his wife. As Job 1:22 summarily said: "In all this, Job did not sin in what he said."

As the greatest man in the East (Job 1:4), Job had a wide circle of friends—both young and matured in age—who revered and respected him. (Job 29:7-20). Yet, as his adversity intensified, he was left in a state of ideological loneliness when his friends intimated that his sufferings were the result of his sins (Job 4-8). Several of the chapters of the book of Job uncovered the prolonged conversations that Job's friends had with him. At the end of the conversations, he was left without what he needed most—care, comfort, and consolation.

The distinction is made between being alone and being lonely. Nothing in the text suggests that Job's wife had physically left him. He was not alone. They were physically in the same space, but spiritually in separate places. The same is true for Job's friends. They were physically in the same place, but ideologically and emotionally distanced. Job was a lonely man!

See the duration of the friends' visits with Job and the length of the conversations that they had with him. That is commendable, for as Chase (2024) stated, "People's presence can be a comfort to those who suffer. Being present shows forethought, concern, and care" (para. 13). But what good is physical presence if there is no emotional and spiritual connection? It is no wonder that individuals can feel lonely even in the physical presence of others.

God's Presence in Lonely Places

If Job felt that he was left by his wife and his friends in a rather lonely place, the posture that he assumed signalled that he was confident of the presence of God, in whom he believed. The second point for consideration, therefore, surrounds the fact of God's presence in places of loneliness.

As the walls of loneliness caved in on Job, he is heard in Job 29 and 30 reaching out to the only source that he had left—the God that he served. In Job 29:1, Job is heard to say, "How I long for the months gone by, for the days when God watched over me ..." In Job 30:20, he further said,

> I cry out to you, O God, but you do not answer; I stand up, but you merely look at me. You turn on me ruthlessly; with the might of your hand, you attack me. You snatch me up and drive me before the wind; you toss me about in the storm. I know you will bring me down to death, to the place appointed for all the living.

Although the answer from God was not forthcoming immediately, Job continued to call out to Him. This indicated Job's confidence in God's abiding presence and the assurance that He would one day respond, although he did not know when. God's eventual response to Job's cry for help and comfort signals that even in silence, He was intimately aware of Job's difficult experiences of pain, suffering, and loneliness. God's response to Job's pleadings is instructive, as it is comforting, and is the third point of focus in this reflection.

God's Response to a Lonely Heart

God's response to Job is recorded in Job 38:1. "Then the Lord answered Job out of the storm. He said, 'Who is this that darkens my counsel with words without knowledge? Brace yourself like a man; I will question you, and you shall answer me." In the slate of questions, God revealed to Job the splendour of the universe, the might of His hand in the creation of all things, and the extent of His dominion over all of creation. God's response evidently transformed Job's life and helped him return from the place of loneliness.

Returning from a Lonely Place

In Job 42:1-6, Job is heard to have said to God:

> I know that you can do all things; no plan of yours can be thwarted. You asked, 'Who is this that obscures my counsel without knowledge?' Surely, I spoke of things I did not understand, things too wonderful for me to know. My ears had heard of you, but now my eyes have seen you. Therefore, I despise myself and repent in dust and ashes.

God's response to Job's pleas evidently transformed Job's posture and perspective. In the light of God's greatness and glory, Job assumed a posture of silence and humility before the Almighty God. Job was a mere nobody before God, who was everything in every way. No longer did Job want to speak; for, in fact, he had nothing to say to a God who had everything to say. The revelations of God plunged Job into deep spiritual submission and humility.

Job also experienced a change of perspective as he came to realize that he did not truly know God in His fullness. Of course, he revered and honoured God in the past. But, as he listened to God and contemplated His wonderful acts as they were displayed before him, he came to realize that his a priori knowledge of God was limited—there was much more to God than he thought he knew or had previously experienced.

The importance that was accorded to Job by his countrymen and that he also accorded himself in the past, was now obliterated, as he stood before the God of majestic splendour. Job came to realize that since God was the Sovereign Creator of all things and Sovereign Ruler of all things, the most that he, Job, could do despite his pain and suffering was to submit to the will of the Almighty God.

Job emerged from a place of loneliness as a completely changed person. This change may not have been realized had he not experienced those difficult days of loneliness. From a place of aloneness and loneliness, Job was awakened to the awesome presence of his God. Out of the loneliness of his moments, Job came to find the God who reigns supremely over all.

I can almost hear Job, like David, saying, "It was good for me to be afflicted so that I may learn your decrees" (Psalm 119:71). Job's encounter with God completely changed his life. For he came to realize that God was not as absent or as far away as he thought. The presence of a God who speaks to a lonely heart must have silenced Job for the only posture that he assumed was one of quietude and admiration for the God who presents Himself to a lonely heart.

Positioning to Stand Firm

Are you experiencing difficult days of loneliness? The spate of illness that is now your reality may have left you in a lonely place. No one understands the intensity of the pain and the frustration resulting from the limitations of the medical interventions. The visits of family, friends, and well-wishers have decreased, and their words of encouragement are not enough to remove the blanket of loneliness that traps your thoughts. You have been left in a difficult place of loneliness.

Illness may not be what has placed you in a lonely place. Taking a stand for what is right in the workplace could leave you in a lonely place. You could be the lone voice in the community, breaking the culture of silence to address injustice. That, too, can pull you into a very lonely place. The question, though, is, what is the posture that you assume in your difficult place of loneliness?

Irrespective of what has occasioned your being in a lonely place, pattern Job's example and call out to God repeatedly and unreservedly. Rest assured that the omnipotent, omnipresent, and omniscient God sees you in that lonely place. He is not in the far distance as some may want you to think! He is with you and is mindful of the loneliness that has become your lived experience. Go ahead and talk to God. He may not respond with immediacy, but He is there. Constantly remind yourself of Jesus' promise to all who follow Him: "… And surely I am with you always, to the very end of the age" (Matthew 28:20). Encourage yourself as you wait for God to make His transformative presence felt right there in your lonely place.

4.

Difficult Days of Infertility

St. Luke 1:1-16

The beautiful young couple celebrated their 12th wedding anniversary with a sense of accomplishment and gratitude to God for having helped them to hurdle the "teething pains" of marriage. Professionally, they were both successful. Socially, they had a wide circle of friends and familial support. Spiritually, they had matured in the faith and served as the leaders for the couples' ministry in their local church. Although they were content with their lives, there was a deep longing in their heart for a child.

Difficult days were as much a part of the experience of believers in the New Testament as they were for believers in the Old Testament. St. Luke chapter 1:1-16 is the passage of focus in this chapter. The passage records the story of a priest named Zechariah and Elizabeth, his wife. They were both in right standing with God. Yet, they were faced with one of the most difficult experiences of their day. Their story reiterates the point that even believers with a good report will experience difficult days.

Challenged Despite a Good Report

A profile of Zechariah and Elizabeth, this good and godly couple, is presented in St. Luke 1:5-6.

> In the time of Herod, king of Judea, there was a priest named Zachariah, who belonged to the priestly division of Abijah; his wife, Elizabeth, was also a descendant of Aaron. Both of them were upright in the sight of God, observing all the Lord's commandments and regulations blamelessly. But they had no children, because Elizabeth was barren, and they were both well along in years.

It was considered a reproach for a woman to be unable to have children. She was regarded as being less than other women. She was stigmatized, mocked, and jeered, and was the target of unkind conversation. This state of being barren must have been discomfiting for Elizabeth. Other women experienced the joy of caring for their children, of hearing them say their first words or take their first steps, but not Elizabeth.

Along with praying, Elizabeth must have done everything humanly possible to try to conceive and change her status. But she remained barren. She must have felt a sense of hopelessness as her prayers remained unanswered and the window of opportunity for conceiving closed upon her.

Being without a child must also have been a difficult experience for Zechariah. He must have shared his wife's frustration and disappointment as they tried, without success, to conceive. Other men took their children to the temple to be blessed; Zechariah never had that opportunity. Other men had the honoured privilege of naming their children, not Zechariah. Other men had sons who would have carried on their names. That would not have been Zechariah's experience.

Although this righteous priest and his equally righteous wife were overtaken by the challenge of infertility, Zechariah assumed a posture of commitment to his call to be a priest. When it was his turn to serve in the temple, Zechariah positioned himself to fulfil his priestly duties. This matter becomes the second point of focus.

Commitment to Duty

St. Luke 1:8-10 paints the captivating picture of Zechariah's commitment to duty.

> Once when Zechariah's division was on duty and he was serving as priest before God, he was chosen by lot, according to the custom of the priesthood, to go into the temple of the Lord and burn incense. And when the time for the burning of incense came, all the assembled worshippers were praying outside.

Bible commentators inform that, because there was a great number of priests, performing the special daily duty of burning incense in the temple was a once-in-a-lifetime opportunity granted to each priest; some never had the opportunity (Marshall, 1970).

One gets the sense that Zechariah highly esteemed his call to be a priest. He had reason to be disappointed with life, but he was still a priest with high regard for his God and deep commitment to his call. He was never going to be a father, but he was not going to miss the opportunity to serve as priest in the temple. When it was Zechariah's time to serve in the temple, he faithfully positioned himself at the altar of incense to do what he was called by God to do.

Visitation at the Place of Occupation.

Zechariah's posture of commitment to his godly assignment brings into focus a third point: the visitation at the place of occupation. According to Luke 1:11,

> ... an angel of the Lord appeared to him standing at the right side of the altar of incense, ... When Zechariah saw him, he was startled and was gripped with fear. But the angel said to him: "Do not be afraid Zechariah, your prayer has been heard. Your wife Elizabeth will bear you a son, and you are to give him the name John."

It is not a small matter that this holy visitation occurred while Zechariah was faithfully fulfilling his priestly duties. Seemingly, this was nothing short of God's recognition and endorsement of Zechariah's high regard for his call to ministry, and of his faithfulness in service to his God. In this scenario, it is abundantly clear that heaven takes note of what happens on earth. God takes note of the posture that his people assume during difficult experiences. Clearly, God took note of the posture that Zechariah assumed in his difficult situation. But there is a fourth matter to which the reflections in this chapter give attention.

Purpose in Delay

Zechariah's prayers were not answered when he expected. That was because God had bigger and better things in store for him and his godly wife, Elizabeth. Zechariah was merely asking for a son, but any other son born to Zechariah and Elizabeth at any other time would not have been the same son that God had in mind. The child that God had in mind for them was no ordinary child! As Luke Chapter 1:14-17 tells us,

> He will be a joy and delight to you, and many will rejoice at his birth, for he will be great in the sight of the Lord. ... He will be filled with the Holy Spirit even from birth. ... And he will go on before the Lord in the spirit and power of Elijah ... to make ready a people prepared for the Lord.

A child of the described order was worth every ounce of the couple's shame and every minute of their wait.

Positioning to Stand Firm

We sometimes become disappointed when our prayers are not answered in the ways or at the times we expect. However, it is helpful to know that God is pleased to answer prayers. Where answers are delayed, it could very well be that the thing that we so feverishly desire and about which we fervently pray may not be in the will of God for us. Even if it were, the issue could be with the timing.

We do well to remind ourselves that God's plan and purpose for our lives far outweigh what we desire for ourselves. If we were to go ahead of God and make our own arrangements, the result may be the ordinary, when God's plan was for the extraordinary.

How, then, should we posture in the face of delayed answers to our prayers? If we have sufficiently prayed about the matter that is of concern, we can be assured that our prayer has already been heard. The delayed answer does not mean that God did not hear us the first time that the matter was brought to His attention. In fact, because God is omniscient, He is aware of matters that concern us even before we bring them to His attention!

The best approach in circumstances of God's seeming delayed response to our concerns is to wait. Of course, waiting does not equate to inactivity. As you leave the matter at the Throne of Grace, continue with the business of living, and with the business of serving people, and of serving God.

Let Zechariah's experience and approach to his call remind us that God is taking note! Our faithfulness to God and to His work is what matters. Commitment to the cause advances the kingdom of God and brings praise to the precious name of Jesus.

5.

Difficult Days of Doubt

St. Luke 1:14-17; Matthew 3:1-11; Matthew 11:5-6

Mother Grey, as she was affectionately called, had been a believer for over 60 years. She lived an exemplary life of faithful service to God and her community. Yet, as the curtains came down on her life at 101 years old, she seemed to have needed the reassurance that her name was written in the Lamb's Book of Life.

St. Luke 1:14-17, Matthew 3:1-11, and Matthew 11:5-6 are the passages of focus in this chapter. The passages account for the life and ministry of John the Baptist, who was the forerunner of Christ Jesus. John's experience underscores the fact that those who have come to faith in Christ Jesus and faithfully serve the Lord will also experience difficult days. An appreciation of the extent of John's ministry sets the stage for an understanding of the seemingly difficult days of doubt that became his reality.

The Extent of John's Ministry

John was born to a priest of the day named Zechariah and his wife, Elizabeth. Seemingly, the couple had earnestly asked God for a child. However, that prayer was not answered until the couple were well advanced in age. Luke 1:14-17 recounts the story of the angel who visited Zechariah while he was serving in the temple. The angel informed him that his prayer for a child was answered and outlined to him the purpose of the child's life.

> He will be a joy and delight to you, and many will rejoice because of his birth, for he will be great in the sight of the Lord. He is never to take wine or other fermented drink, and he will be filled with the Holy Spirit even before he is born. He will bring back many of the people of Israel to the Lord their God. And he will go on before the Lord, in the spirit and power of Elijah, to turn the hearts of the parents to their children and the disobedient

to the wisdom of the righteous—to make ready a people prepared for the Lord.

True to the purpose for which he was born, John, "...went into all the country around the Jordan, preaching a baptism of repentance for the forgiveness of sins (Luke 3:3). The Spirit of the Lord was evident in John's ministry. He was fierce and fearless in his delivery and in his responses to those who questioned his person and the authority behind his preaching.

> But when he saw many of the Pharisees and Sadducees coming to where he was baptizing, he said to them: "You brood of vipers! Who warned you to flee from the coming wrath? Produce fruit in keeping with repentance. And do not think you can say to yourselves, 'We have Abraham as our father.' I tell you that out of these stones God can raise up children for Abraham. The axe is already at the root of the trees, and every tree that does not produce good fruit will be cut down and thrown into the fire. (Matthew 3:10)

John was careful to point out that he was not the Messiah. In Matthew 3:11, he is heard to have said,

I baptize you with water for repentance. But after me comes one who is more powerful than I, whose sandals I am not worthy to carry. He will baptize you with the Holy Spirit and fire. His winnowing fork is in his hand, and he will clear his threshing floor, gathering his wheat into the barn and burning up the chaff with unquenchable fire.

By the same token, John spared no moment to point his listeners to Jesus with the words, "Behold the Lamb of God who takes away the sins of the world" (John 1:29). There should be no mistaking him for the Christ who was the One who would redeem the world. John also took no issue when, on one occasion, he pointed his disciples to Jesus, the Lamb of God, and they left him to follow Jesus. John knew the subordination of his place and the exaltation of Jesus.

It was clear that John had the ministry to which he was called at heart. He spared no punches in exposing the socio-political ills of the day, wherever and by whomever they were committed. It was in this vein that he had exposed the shenanigans of the king, including the fact that he had taken his brother's wife (Luke 3:19-20). Neither the king nor the queen took kindly to the exposure.

To quieten John, the king ordered his imprisonment, where the threat of death hung loosely over his head.

Considering John's high calling and the approach that he took in fulfilling his calling and purpose, the impact that imprisonment and the threat of death had on him is of great interest and will be examined.

The Effects of Threat

The interminable days of isolation and the threat of death that John, the firebrand preacher, experienced in prison may have caused clouds of doubt about Jesus' authenticity to have hovered over his mind. As Matthew 11:3 records, "When John, who was in prison, heard about the deeds of the Messiah, he sent his disciples to ask Him, 'Are you the one who is to come, or should we expect someone else?'" (Matthew 11:2).

The single question that John asked seems to be loaded with several other questions. If Jesus were "the One" who would deliver the people from the evil rulers of the day and set the prisoners free, then why had He not done anything about John's unjust imprisonment? Where did John's release fit into the scheme of things? Apart from the political undertone of the question, there was also a familial reality in view.

John's mother was a relative of Jesus' mother (Luke 1:16). Should this familial connection not inspire Jesus, "the One," to have intervened on John's behalf? John's perception could very well be that while Jesus was in the community helping others, His very own cousin languished in prison with the threat of death hanging over his head. Jesus' indirect response to John's question was simple and straightforward. His response brings a third matter into sharp focus.

Jesus' Empathetic Response

The question that John sent his disciples to ask Jesus was not lost on Jesus. He heard John's heart and understood even what was not vocalized. In a moment of exemplary sensitivity to the delicacy of the question, Jesus conveyed a message to John through the disciples who had been sent with the question.

> Go back and report to John what you hear and see: The blind receive sight, the lame walk, those who have leprosy are cleansed, the deaf hear, the dead are raised, and the good news is proclaimed to the poor. Blessed is the man who does not fall away on account of me. (Matthew 11:5-6)

Jesus' response to John's question was filled with empathy. He clearly understood that this was a defining moment for both John and John's disciples. The question of the Messiah needed to have been settled once and for all for both John and his disciples. John was about to be executed. He needed to know that even in the face of that difficult moment, Jesus was the Christ.

The bearers of the question also needed to know beyond doubt that Jesus was, in fact, the Messiah, regardless of life's circumstances. John had earlier pointed to Jesus and informed his disciples that He was the "Lamb of God who takes away the sin of the world" (John 1:29). At this critical juncture, there should be no question in the minds of John's disciples about Jesus.

If John and his disciples were to reflect on the miracles that Jesus had been performing, they would come to realize that these were the very miracles that Isaiah's prophecy said that the Messiah would have performed (Isaiah 61:1-3). Despite the difficult circumstances of the day, that realization would have scattered any lingering clouds of doubt that had arisen on their minds.

However, the question remained as to why a bad thing, imprisonment, had become the reality of the servant of God. The final sentence in Jesus's response to John summarizes an important lesson that Christ-followers must, of necessity, embrace. "Blessed is the man who does not fall away on account of me" (Matthew 11:6). The statement subliminally acknowledges that it is possible for believers to succumb to external pressure and abandon their faith. A blessing is, therefore, conferred on those who stand firm and keep the faith despite the challenges.

The passage does not provide insights into the impact that Jesus' response had on John. However, it is noted that Jesus had nothing disparaging to say about John. His appraisal of John, as He then spoke with the crowd, suggests that John was in a good place despite his seeming moment of doubt. "Truly I tell you, among those born of women there has not risen anyone greater than John the Baptist, yet whoever is least in the kingdom of heaven is greater than he" (Matthew 11:11).

Positioning to Stand Firm

Clouds of doubt are likely to gather in our hearts in the face of unmet expectations. In these circumstances, we ask questions like, "Where was God when I needed Him?" "How could God have allowed that to happen?" These questions are clear indicators that clouds of doubt are beginning to gather in our minds and in our spirits. As reasonable as these questions are, we should also ask ourselves whether our expectations align with God's promises and with His intentions for our lives.

During the difficult days of doubt and unmet expectations, we do well to remind ourselves and each other of the written Word of God that is applicable to the given situation. In these circumstances, times of quiet reflection will be particularly important and beneficial.

Should clouds of doubt ever gather in our minds, we do well to assume a posture of unswerving faith in the promises of God. We do well to remember that God is faithful to do all that He promised. Instead of asking, "Where is God when I need him?" let us ask ourselves, "What has God said about this situation?" or "What is God saying in this situation?" Be reminded that the Word of God has an answer for every question that we could possibly have.

The days may be dark and dismal, but God said He would be with us always, and that includes during our difficult days. The circumstances may be trying and tiring, but God said He would give grace to the weary (Isaiah 40:29). Choosing to believe the Word of God pushes back the clouds of doubt and reveals God's faithfulness.

6.

Difficult Days of Disappointment

Luke 24:13-34

D isappointment is among the worst of human experiences. This emotion is usually indicated by the expressions, "I thought that ..." or "I hoped that ..." It is generally believed that disappointment is the result of unmet expectations. Therefore, to avoid being disappointed, the advice given by some is that expectations be lowered. Whether this is good counsel is debatable for even low expectations can result in a degree of disappointment.

Luke 24:13-34 is the passage of focus in this chapter. The passage brings to our attention the wave of disappointment that swept over Jesus' disciples who had witnessed his death and burial. The chapter puts the disciples' experience in context and considers three matters of interest, the first being the place of pain.

The Place of Pain

Prior to His crucifixion, Jesus gave His disciples the strict command: "Do not leave Jerusalem, but wait for the gift my Father promised, which you have heard me speak about. For John baptized with water, but in a few days you will be baptized with the Holy Spirit" (Acts 1:4-5). However, as the events unfolded, Jesus' words seemed to have been lost on the disciples—at least on two of the disciples to whom Jesus appeared after his resurrection.

Contrary to Jesus' instructions, these two men were returning to their home in Emmaus, a village outside of Jerusalem. Along the way, "They were talking with each other about everything that had happened. As they talked and discussed these things with each other, Jesus himself came up and walked along with them; but they were kept from recognizing him" (Luke 24:15-16).

The men's disappointment was palpable. They were tired of the tyranny that marked the reign of the kings of the day. They longed for the redemption of Israel and believed that it would have been realized by Jesus. The men's hopes were dashed to pieces as they looked at Jesus' limp body hanging from the cross.

The men's leaving Jerusalem suggests that they may have feared being similarly arrested and crucified. Jesus' instruction that the disciples should remain in Jerusalem did not hold out much hope for them. Their hope for deliverance was shattered, and they were crestfallen. No wonder they journeyed away from Jerusalem, for it had become the place of pain—not the place of promise about which Jesus spoke.

A Picture of Disappointment

Jesus joined the men's conversation and asked, "What are you discussing together as you walk along?" Of course, Jesus knew what the topic of the men's discussion was. However, His question signalled that He was mindful that the men were emotionally distraught because of the circumstances of the day, and He cared.

There was also something strategic about Jesus' question. It gained Him an entrance into the conversation that the men were having about the crucifixion. Entrance into the conversation provided Jesus with the opportunity to explain the occurrences of the day, and, therefore, change the narrative that only served to plunge the men further into the shadows of gloom.

There is something about disappointment that is easily detected in one's demeanour and words. For the two men who had retreated from the place of pain, their body language and the tone of their voices as they responded to Jesus' question revealed the disappointment that had engulfed their hearts.

They stood still, their faces downcast. One of them, named Cleopas, asked him, "Are you only a visitor to Jerusalem and does not know the things that have happened there in these days? 'What things?' he asked. 'About Jesus of Nazareth,' they replied. He was a prophet, powerful in word and deed before God and all the people. The chief priests and our rulers handed him over to be sentenced to death, and they crucified him. (Luke 24:17, 18)

Luke 24:20-24 is the most revealing of the men's conversation.

But we had hoped that he was the one who was going to redeem Israel. And what is more, it is the third day since all this took place. In addition, some of our women amazed us. They went to the tomb early this morning but didn't find his body. They came and told us that they had seen a vision of angels who said he was alive. Then some of our companions went to the tomb and found it just as the women had said, but him they did not see.

Attention is called to the extent to which Jesus allowed the men to unburden their souls to Him, although they perceived Him to be a stranger. Perhaps it was easy for them to unburden their souls to a stranger. Perhaps they found it therapeutic to simply "get it off their chest" to anyone who would listen. Perhaps they simply needed someone to understand the depth of their pain and disappointment.

Regardless of the reason for the men's detailed recounting of the events that took place earlier in the day, the fact that Jesus journeyed with the men while they emptied themselves of the pain in their hearts is worthy of note and brings into focus the third matter for consideration.

The Pace of Patience

The men's account of the events that unfolded was quite detailed. But Jesus had no intention to hurry them along. He knew that they were misguided in the facts, yet He patiently listened. He had other matters to attend to before returning to His Father, but these two men also needed his attention. These two disciples, with a sense of disappointment in their hearts, needed a moment with the "Friend of a wounded heart." Jesus was prepared to listen to the men for as long as they felt the need to unburden their souls and relieve their minds of the circumstances that had caused them the extent of disappointment.

Jesus only interrupted the men's long discourse after He had listened long enough. At the appropriate time, He then said, "How foolish you are, and how slow to believe all that the prophets have spoken! Did not the Messiah have to suffer these things and then enter his glory?" (Luke 24:25, 26). Jesus knew that their disappointment was rooted in their misperception of what had transpired in Jerusalem. He therefore took the time to correct their misperception and help them gain perspective.

If Jesus' initial response to the despondent men was a sharp rebuke, the words that followed were a sterling display of unparalleled patience and kindness. According to verse 27, "… beginning with Moses and all the Prophets, he explained to them what was said in all the Scriptures concerning himself" (Luke 24:27).

There is credence to the notion that learning has not taken place unless there is behaviour change. The information that Jesus shared was certainly not new to the men. Their challenge, however, was their inability to relate the historical content to the current context; to translate knowledge into behaviour.

Despite Jesus' patient explanation of the circumstances that had caused the men their heartbreak, they did not recognize that it was Jesus who was walking and talking with them the full distance to their village.

The men eventually arrived at their home. By then, their pain would have been sufficiently soothed, and they would have been in a renewed emotional state. The end of their destination may, therefore, have brought the conversation to a close. But what of the "stranger" who had helped them to gain perspective about the circumstances of the day? The actions of the men, as outlined in Luke 24:28, highlight a pivotal principle.

The Principle of Hospitality

According to Luke 24:28,

> As they approached the village to which they were going, Jesus continued as if he were going farther. But they urged him strongly, "Stay with us, for it is nearly evening; the day is almost over." So he went in to stay with them.

The perceived "stranger" who patiently listened to the men's lamentations of woe and detailed expressions of disappointment still had a distance to go. Considering the distance they had been travelling and the time of the day, the men perceived that the "stranger" could surely benefit from a place in which to refresh himself and rest before proceeding on his journey. With keen awareness of the needs of the "stranger", the men seized the opportunity to exercise the

ZOE M. SIMPSON

principle of hospitality. The difficult experience that the men had did not leave them bereft of the need to rise to the occasion and demonstrate good practice. Good for them! Their act of generosity set the stage for the risen Christ to be revealed to them.

Change of Perspective

Jesus evidently accepted the men's invitation to stay the night in their home. A meal was served, and they all sat at the table to partake. The posture that the "stranger" assumed at the table is revelatory of his authority. According to Luke 24:30-31, "when he [Jesus] was at the table with them, he took bread, gave thanks, broke it and began to give it to them. Then their eyes were opened, and they recognized him, and he disappeared from their sight."

If the "stranger's" authority escaped the men when he inserted himself into their conversation and took charge of the situation, it did not escape them when he asserted himself at the table and again took charge of the undertaking. The breaking of bread and giving thanks seemed to have been the signature action of Jesus by which the disciples readily identified Him.

Hear the change of perspective and positionality in the words of the men after their eyes were opened! See the right-about turn that they made back to Jerusalem, the place of pain, but also the place of the Promise! "Were not our hearts burning within us while he talked with us on the road and opened the Scriptures to us?" They got up and returned at once to Jerusalem."

The place of pain was no longer coloured by shades of disappointment for the men. The perceived threat of death was no longer of any moment for them, for they knew that Jesus was alive and well. Things did not turn out as they anticipated in Jerusalem, but all was well. The revelation that Jesus had risen completely changed their perspective on the circumstances that brought about their seeming disappointment.

Jesus disappeared from their sight, but they then knew in their hearts that He was alive! In fact, Jesus was there all the time! Their hearts were sad and broken, but Jesus was there. They did not recognize Him, but He was journeying with them all the way. After all was said and done, the situation that had been the source of the disciples' disappointment was the one that brought them the deliverance they had anticipated.

Positioning to Stand Firm

What is the situation that has left you most disappointed? Perhaps you had high hopes that the investment would yield a substantial financial return. Your expectation did not materialize, and you are very disappointed. Although you upskilled yourself and improved your person and performance, you did not get the anticipated promotion on the job. You are extremely disappointed. After all the praying and fasting, you expected that God would have healed your loved one. You are extremely disappointed because your loved one is still unwell. Your first marriage was a disaster, and you trusted that this one would be better. It was not better, and you are disappointed.

Jesus is mindful of the circumstances that assail and disappoint us. In the difficult circumstances of disappointment, it is helpful to remember that Jesus is right there with us. We cannot physically see Him, but He is walking the distance of the journey of disappointment with us. We may not sense His presence, but He is there just like He said He would: "… And surely I am with you always, to the very end of the age" (Matthew 28:20).

It is also helpful to examine our perceptions. Things are not always what they seem. Similarly, things are not as bad as they seem. Quite often, if we were to change the lenses through which we look at our circumstances, we would come to realize that the things that happen to us are working for our good and for God's glory. The most salient question to be asked, therefore, is: Do we trust God to fulfil His promises to us?

Additionally, we should be careful to examine our expectations and ask ourselves the pertinent questions: What was the basis of my expectations? Were my expectations based on false premises or on the promises of God? Were my expectations unrealistic?

We invite disappointment into our lives when our expectations are not grounded in the promises of God. We expose ourselves to disappointment when we misinterpret or misunderstand what God says. The challenge, therefore, is to know with certainty what God says about our situations. We can acquire this knowledge through the written Word of God. We should be careful to read and gain the correct understanding of the Word and base our expectations solely on what God says.

7.

Difficult Days of Missteps

2nd Corinthians 2:5-11

To admit that even the most devout believer may fall into sin is to correctly understand that it is Satan's plan for each believer to depart from the faith. Falling into sin sets the stage for difficult days for the individual as much as for the community of believers. The body of believers may find it challenging to forgive the individual, and the individual may likewise struggle to forgive themselves.

2 Corinthians 2:5-11 is the passage of focus for this chapter, which addresses the difficult experience of falling into sin. The passage recounts the response of the body of believers in Corinth to a brother who had fallen into sin and advances an appropriate model that should be applied in this difficult circumstance.

The Weight of the Discipline

The first consideration concerns the weight of the discipline. In addressing the issue, Paul carefully pointed out that, "if anyone has caused grief, he has not so much grieved me as he has grieved all of you.... The punishment inflicted on him by the majority is sufficient for him" 2 Corinthians 2:5). The indication is that the sin that the individual committed had become common knowledge, and a concerted decision was made to discipline him.

Disciplining the brother certainly had its place. It would send an unequivocal message that his action was impermissible to the Christian faith. Disciplining the brother would also send a strong message to other believers that such an action was intolerable, and they should not even consider it.

Additionally, disciplining the brother would indicate to the unbelievers that the act committed was incongruent with the Christian faith and would not be condoned. The issue, however, was that the extent of the discipline outweighed the act that was committed. Paul, therefore, wanted the believers to know that "enough is enough" and issued the instructions to halt the course of discipline.

The instruction to halt the discipline that was being administered was predicated on the fact that the brother had demonstrated sorrow for his actions and repentance of heart.

In the circumstance, it was now for the body of believers to walk the brother back into fellowship.

The Way to Treat the Brother

According to 2 Corinthians 2:7-8, "Now instead, you ought to forgive and comfort him, so that he will not be overwhelmed by excessive sorrow. I urge you, therefore, to reaffirm your love for him." The verses indicate a 3-tiered approach to be taken. First and foremost, it was essential for the community of believers to forgive the brother. Leave the past behind and move on together. Second, the body of believers should comfort the brother and reassure him of his place within the body. Third, the body of believers should demonstrate love to the brother.

In a practical sense, believers should restore those who have erred to their rightful place within the body and continue to demonstrate Christian love toward them. Discipline, where it becomes necessary, should be done in love, with the aim of restoring and strengthening. The consequences of the sinful actions may require appropriate intervention. Where this is the case, others should "walk" beside the offender throughout the intervention, and monitor and praise any progress that is made.

The Wisdom of Restoration

The third consideration surrounds the wisdom of restoration. The instruction to forgive, comfort, and love the erring brother follows in 2 Corinthians 5:11, "Lest Satan should get an advantage of us: for we are not ignorant of his devices." To keep the erring brother out of the body is to expose him to further attacks of the Devil.

To delay his restoration is to leave him prey to falling further into sin. To not hasten his restoration is to deny him the warmth of the fellowship, which is essential to his further spiritual growth and development. Restoration forms a protective hedge that aids the healing process and generates life. There is, therefore, much wisdom in restoring the brother who has fallen into sin to the Christian community.

Positioning to Stand Firm

Who among the body of believers is not susceptible to error? Which of us would not desire to be forgiven and restored if we were to fall into sin? Every believer experienced the forgiveness of sin on the basis of the grace of God—the undeserved favour of God. The very moment we confess and forsake our sin is the moment when God forgives and restores us. It is for us, then, to likewise apply grace and forgive and restore our brothers and sisters if they err.

To not forgive and restore a member who had a misstep is idolatrous—that is playing God to whom alone judgement belongs! Those who do not forgive and restore are pretentious, for that is to behave as though they are beyond making a similar mistake. On the other hand, those who forgive and restore acknowledge the need to extend grace to others as it was similarly extended to them. Those who forgive and restore demonstrate the Christian love that believers are called to have for one another.

The Christian faith is not one of ostracization and condemnation. It is, instead, a faith of restoration, reconciliation, and redemption. Is there one among you who erred? The discipline that is administered must include measures to help the believer strengthen their weak areas.

Discipline must be instructive and corrective, or else it becomes destructive. The Christlike practice is for those who are strong to walk beside those who are weak, helping them put measures in place to prevent mistakes in the future. The call is for us to look beyond the offence and see the heart of the brother and the sister who needs to be supported to stand firm in their faith.

8.

Difficult Days of Imprisonment I

Philippians 1:1-2

T he fledgling moderator began his opening remarks at a function that I attended with the unexpected statement, "I want a title!" He then explained that some persons seem to be overly preoccupied with their titles and will be offended if they are not addressed accordingly. The brother, therefore, concluded that having a title had its merits.

The inordinate preoccupation with titles is indicative of the sense of importance that some people accord themselves. The reflections in this chapter examine the extent to which Paul's perception of himself and of the One to whom he belonged helped him navigate the difficult days of imprisonment. The reflections are grounded in Philippians 1:1-2, from which three observations are made, the first being the Apostle's self-perception as a servant.

Perceiving Self as a Servant

The letter to the Philippians was written while the Apostle Paul was in prison in Rome. The letter begins with the simple yet insightful introduction: "Paul and Timothy, servants of the Lord Jesus, ..." (Philippians 1:1a).

Bible scholars inform that Paul was well-read and well-educated. Yet, there is nothing in the introductory statement of the letter that mentions or even alludes to Paul's qualifications or the important titles that he had. Clearly, he was not preoccupied with his abilities; neither did he allow his qualifications to colour his self-perception. In Paul's estimation, he was only a servant, a slave of the Lord Jesus Christ.

Paul's perception of himself as a servant draws attention to the posture of humility and duty that he assumed. A servant has nothing to call his own, not even his life. A servant is at his master's disposal and is under obligation to deliver on the desires and dictates of his master. For Paul to perceive himself as a servant indicates that he had relinquished himself of reputation and rights and handed them to his Master.

The posture of humility and duty that Paul assumed also draws attention to the subordinate position he gratefully occupied. Servants position themselves behind their masters, but never beside or in front of them. It was with this awareness that Paul intentionally highlighted the Lordship of Jesus, instead of any accolade that he may have had. Importance was placed solely on his Master and not on him, the servant.

Servants position themselves to serve their master irrespective of prevailing circumstances. It was in that position of duty that Paul, the servant of Jesus Christ, set about writing to the Philippians to encourage them in the faith. Although he was in prison, his commitment to his Master saw him carrying out his assignment with no less fervour than if he were free. He was physically bound, but his freedom of spirit fuelled his passion to faithfully serve his Master.

The posture of humility that Paul assumed is further highlighted in his acknowledgement of Timothy, his protégé, as a fellow servant of the Lord Jesus Christ. Paul was the one commissioned by God to preach the Gospel, and he was the author of the letter. However, Timothy would have helped him in one way or another. Therefore, Paul humbly accorded equal credit to another servant of the Lord Jesus.

The picture painted in Paul's introductory statement is that he, alongside his protégé, was a humble servant of the Lord Jesus, dutifully fulfilling the mandate of preaching the gospel.

Perceiving Jesus as Lord and Master

If Paul rightly perceived himself as a servant, he also rightly perceived Jesus as Lord. To ascribe Lordship to Jesus is to admit that He is the supreme authority and ruler over everything. It was this Jesus to whom Paul belonged, to whom he had resigned himself, and under whose authority he gladly served. Being a servant of the Lord Jesus guarantees His servant an immense sense of security.

It is no wonder, therefore, that Paul's introduction of himself as a servant of the Lord Jesus rings with an undisturbed knowing that no matter where his assignment took him, or what befell him, his Master, who rules and reigns over everything with supreme authority, would also rule and reign over all the circumstances of his life. Regardless of the circumstances of his life, all would be well. His only preoccupation and passion were to faithfully serve his Master and complete the tasks assigned to him.

Prioritizing Service to Jesus

As a servant of the Lord Jesus, Paul was consumed by and preoccupied with his assignment to preach the Gospel to the Gentiles. He referenced this assignment in passages such as Acts 9:15, Galatians 1:9, Ephesians 3:1-12, and 2 Timothy

1:11. Paul was also endued with a passion to fulfil his assignment. Picture him, therefore, sitting in prison, focused on continuing to do the work of his Lord and Master; serving the believers in Philippi; quite content to know that he was only a servant; a servant of the Lord Jesus Christ.

Prison of whatever description is not the ideal place. Imprisonment would have brought Paul a plethora of issues about which he could complain, but servants serve; they do not complain. He could have called it quits, but servants remain faithful to the cause. It was with this resolute posture and the correct perception of who he was and to whom he belonged that Paul continued to fulfil his God-given mandate to preach the good news of salvation through Jesus from the confines of prison.

Positioning to Stand Firm

As a follower of Christ Jesus, how do you perceive yourself? How do you perceive Jesus? Take a moment today to examine and clarify your perception of yourself and of Jesus. The posture you assume during challenging circumstances is influenced by how you perceive yourself as well as how you perceive Christ Jesus.

Believers sometimes ask, 'Why should servants of the Lord suffer so much pain?' Where is God when it hurts so very much? In trying circumstances, it is helpful to accept that you are a servant of the Lord Jesus Christ. As such, you are at his disposal and discretion. Do not entertain the thought of quitting; that is not what faithful servants do!

Take comfort in knowing that you are in God's will and that He will not give you more than you can bear. Remind yourself of God's promise to be with you always (Matthew 28:20); that includes during your difficult days. The timing for God's intervention in your circumstance may not be what you expect, but God will address the matters of concern in His time and in His way. Will yourself to wait patiently for God's timing and persevere despite the challenges.

Remind yourself, also, that you are a servant of Christ Jesus, who is a good Master—a good Master who is aware of and addresses the welfare and well-being of His servants. This wholesome perception of yourself, as well as your knowledge of the One who is your Master, will help you to stand firm and keep the faith during your difficult days.

9.

Difficult Days of Imprisonment II

Philippians 1:1b-7; Philippians 4:4-7

I listened keenly as my friend shared her story of having been diagnosed with cancer, and I soon understood why she seemed to wear a permanent smile on her face. As her story goes, a wave of negative thoughts initially swept over her. However, she braced herself for the "journey" and went to the Lord in prayer. Her most salient request of the Lord was that He fill her with joy throughout the experience.

The letter to the Philippians was written from Rome, where the Apostle Paul was imprisoned. He was diligently seeking to fulfil his God-given mandate to take the Gospel of Jesus to the Gentile world. Roman officials, however, were vehemently opposed to the Gospel message and the extent to which it was being spread throughout the various territories. Reasons were found to have Paul imprisoned, with the intention of prohibiting the spread of the Gospel.

Philippians 1:1-7 and Philippians 4:4-7 are the passages of focus for this chapter. The passages highlight three observations, the first being the extent to which Paul remained faithful to the call despite the difficult days of imprisonment.

Faithful to the Call

Paul began the letter to the Philippians by acknowledging himself and Timothy, who was his ministry assistant. He then directly addressed the believers in Philippians with the most endearing salutation:

> To all God's holy people in Christ Jesus at Philippi, together with the overseers and deacons Grace and peace to you from God our Father and the Lord Jesus Christ. (Philippians 1:1b-2)

Although Paul's imprisonment was tantamount to a house arrest, he was under surveillance by Roman soldiers who constantly monitored his movements. He was not free to go about his daily life and living, and was denied the opportunity to participate in his usual ministerial course of activities, chief among which was visiting the newly formed churches, where he would encourage the believers in their newfound faith.

The conditions of imprisonment were dislocating and discomfiting to a man whose heart was set on attending to the business of the Lord. Therefore, for Paul to have written this letter to the Philippians under the conditions of imprisonment signals the extent to which he resolutely defied the prohibitions to continue the work to which he was called.

Soldiers may have bound Paul's feet with chains, but they certainly could not bind his spirit. The chains that were around his feet were certainly not around his spirit. The walls of the prison did not prohibit Paul from fulfilling the cause to which he was called. Paul assumed a posture of resilience and used his pen to take him to the places where his feet prevented him.

Focus on the Cause

The imprisonment and the attendant discomforts could have elicited from Paul a bout of bitter complaining. He could have felt immensely sorry for himself and bemoaned the lot that befell him. Paul could have spent the time beseeching the Lord for his release. He could have spent the time strategizing and penning his defence. He could have written to the churches, calling attention to the direness of his situation, seeking their sympathy and support. Paul could have taken any of these justifiable options during this time of confinement, but that was not the case. He chose, instead, to focus on the worthy cause for which he was imprisoned, not on the difficult circumstances of imprisonment. Hence, the letter of encouragement to the believers of the Philippian church.

The letter to the Philippians is said to be the most personal letter written by the Apostle Paul. It was apparent that there was a special place in his heart for the believers who had come to faith during his second missionary journey. The believers practised their faith in a rather hostile environment and needed to be supported. Therefore, despite his own challenges, Paul kept the focus on the cause and wrote to encourage the believers to remain steadfast in their faith during the difficult times.

Overflowing with Joy

A third observation about the posture Paul assumed during his imprisonment surrounds his expressions of joy and the call he made to believers to rejoice always. He wrote in Philippians 1:4-6,

> In all my prayers for all of you, I always pray with joy because of your partnership in the Gospel from the first day until now, being

confident of this, that he who began a good
work in you will carry it on to completion
until the day of Christ Jesus.

For Paul to have been praying for the believers during
the difficult days of imprisonment was one thing. But, for
him to have been praying with joy was quite another! The
indication is that during the difficult days of imprisonment,
Paul had tapped into the divine source of abundant joy.

We know from Galatians 4:22 that joy is a fruit of the
Spirit. As such, joy emanates from the Holy Spirit. With the
Holy Spirit's indwelling, the believer is guaranteed a constant
supply of joy, which is described as a deep, abiding
cheerfulness that comes from the assurance of knowing that
we are loved, forgiven, and empowered by God (Global
Disciples, October 30, 2023). "When we tap into the joy of
the Lord, it becomes a source of resilience and endurance"
(Global Disciples, para. 5).

The theme of joy and rejoicing rings with clarity
throughout the letter to the Philippians. Paul spoke of
rejoicing in prayers (4:4), rejoicing in the fruit of his labour
(1:22), and rejoicing in knowing that Christ is being preached
(1:12-18). Because Paul had assumed the posture of rejoicing
even in his difficult days, he was at liberty to encourage the
believers to also rejoice in their difficulties. In Philippians 4:4,
he emphatically wrote, "Rejoice in the Lord always. I will say

it again: Rejoice! Let your gentleness be evident to all. The Lord is near."

The statement, "the Lord is near", may be construed to mean that Christ Jesus is near to believers in spirit, including in difficult experiences. Jesus' comforting presence in difficult experiences is cause for rejoicing. If the statement is construed to mean that Jesus' return is near, that too is cause for rejoicing, for believers can live in hope that their difficult days will one day come to an end.

Positioning to Stand Firm

Believers in Jesus will face challenges that stem from their expression of faith in Christ Jesus. They may also experience difficult days that are akin to life and living, such as unemployment, a high cost of living, financial insufficiencies, disobedient children, contentious neighbours, unreasonable employers, cantankerous coworkers, failing health, old age, and the related challenges.

Trouble has the propensity to pull individuals into self-pity and feelings of distress and depression. You can prevent yourself from being overtaken by these negative emotions by redirecting your focus to joy-producing experiences. Volunteer to be a member of a short-term mission endeavour. Participate in a community or a personal project and experience the joy of serving God through serving others.

It is also helpful to focus on the needs of others rather than your own. Quite often, our own needs pale into insignificance in the face of the grave needs of others. Take the time to identify someone with a need that you can meet. Extend yourself to helping others and rejoice in knowing that God has blessed you with the ability and capacity to make a difference.

In the face of a challenging experience, do not yield to the temptation to "throw in the towel" and walk away from the faith or from your call. That would signal defeat. Instead, be resolute that you will remain faithful to the call and to the cause of the Gospel of Christ Jesus.

Heed the instructions of the Apostle given to the believers in Philippi and rejoice always. Believers have more than enough reasons to be joyful. Rejoice that you are a member of the family of God. Rejoice that God's Holy Spirit lives within you, and He stands ready to help you in all circumstances. Rejoice that your sins are forgiven and that your name is written in heaven (Luke 10:20). Although your circumstances may be undesirable, your joy should remain unshakable.

Cultivate the spirit of joy and rejoicing by singing songs of praise to the Lord (Ephesians 5:19). Engaging in physical exercise and participating in outdoor activities are also means of cultivating a heart of rejoicing. Since the joy of the Lord is the believer's strength, it makes good sense to regularly tap into the Spirit of joy. Romans 15:13 refers to the God of hope who fills us with all joy. Engage in constant conversations with the Lord in prayer. Listen to Him speak to you through His written Word, through others, and through creation, and see how you become filled with joy even during your difficult days.

10.

Gratitude and Thanksgiving

Philippians 1:3-11

My colleague, Patrice (not her real name), invited several of us to join her on a 100-day gratitude challenge. Her daily expressions of gratitude were shared with the world on her Instagram account. Although I readily embraced the challenge, I must admit that I fell short of the 100 days. However, I have since made it a resolve to practise an attitude of gratitude and certainly encourage others to do likewise.

Philippians 1:3-8 is the passage of focus for this chapter. The passage draws attention to the principle of gratitude and thanksgiving that the Apostle Paul practised during his imprisonment. There are three key observations surrounding this principle to be highlighted: the first is that gratitude and thanksgiving flow from the focus of the heart.

Flowing From the Focus of the Heart

In writing the letter to the Philippians, Paul primarily wanted to thank the believers for their support and to encourage them in the faith. Having established the protocols of the letter, he addressed the first objective and said, "I thank my God every time I remember you. In all my prayers for all of you, I always pray with joy because of your partnership in the gospel from the first day until now" (Philippians 1:3-5). These verses loudly expose Paul's heart of gratitude for the believers' support.

Instead of complaining about the challenges of imprisonment, Paul chose to thank God for the believers and their support of his ministry. The indication is that Paul shifted his focus from the things that were working against him to those that were working for him. This is quite an enabling approach!

The words "every time", "all of you", and "always" used in verse 3 of the text highlight the constancy, fluidity, and frequency with which Paul expressed thanks to God for the believers in Philippi. His heart overflowed with gratitude and thanksgiving because he was focused on their having come to faith and their spiritual maturity. He was mindful of their generosity toward him. This, too, was a sign of the believers' spiritual maturity, and it filled Paul's heart with gratitude and thanksgiving.

The Condition of the Heart

The second observation is the condition of Paul's heart. Hear Paul say in Philippians 1:4-9,

> It is right for me to feel this way about all of you, since I have you in my heart; for whether I am in chains or defending and confirming the Gospel, all of you share in God's grace with me.

The posture of thanksgiving that Paul assumed in this context indicates that his heart was in the right place. He knew that expressing thanks for the believers was the right thing to do. He did not take their support for granted. He was mindful that the Philippian believers were not people of means, and so they would have given from their own meagre supplies. He was mindful that they themselves were experiencing difficult days, yet they continued to support him during his difficult days. Paul did not take the believers for granted, and he wanted them to know that he was mindful of their sacrifice and that he constantly gave thanks to God for them.

To the extent that Paul was thankful for the believers in Philippi, he referred to them as "partners in the ministry." They were not always physically present with him, but they maintained contact vicariously and made every effort to meet his needs. His being in prison was no exception. Paul held the support he received from the believers in high regard and spared no moment to express thanks to God for them.

The Concern of the Heart

Paul was mindful of the trying conditions under which the believers practised their faith. Therefore, his expressions of gratitude and thanksgiving to God for them were accompanied by prayers for their continued growth and maturity. The content of the prayer rightly reveals the concern of Paul's heart.

> And this is my prayer for you: that your love may abound more and more in knowledge and depth of insight, so that you may be able to discern what is best and may be pure and blameless until the day of Christ, filled with the fruit of righteousness that comes through Jesus Christ—to the glory and praise of God. (Philippians 1:9-11)

Paul's prayer was nothing about himself or his difficult situation. It would have been quite understandable if Paul were praying for himself. For there were, in fact, a multiplicity of personal matters about which he could have been praying. He could have been beseeching God for his release from prison, for provisions for his many needs, and for protection from possible danger in the prison. That was not the case! This prayer was not centred on Paul and his needs. This was a prayer entirely and solely centred on the Philippians.

The Philippians faced severe external and internal challenges. These could have derailed and dwarfed their spiritual growth. Paul was, therefore, mindful to pray that the believers grow from strength to strength in the Lord; that they increase in knowledge and in understanding in the way of the Lord; that they come to spiritual maturity and so remain pure and blameless in the way. The spiritual growth and development of the believers was the sole concern of Paul's heart during the difficult days of imprisonment.

Positioning to Stand Firm

This chapter challenges believers to normalise gratitude and thanksgiving as a way of life. If you were to stop and reflect on your life, you would soon realize that there are innumerable things for which to be thankful—little things and big things. You may not be able to purchase the usual supply of food items, but be thankful that you have something to eat. You did not receive the anticipated salary increase, but you still have a job; be grateful for that. Your health is failing as you age, but you are still alive. Be thankful for life! Things could be worse than they are! Do not hesitate to express gratitude and to give thanks to God.

The chapter further invites us to assume a posture of prayer even as we face our difficult days. Prayer does not have to be long or loud. Prayer does not have to be confined to a specific place or time. Importantly, prayer should not only be about us; we must extend our prayers to others. Believers should refrain from pitying themselves and instead pray for the other believers who are also facing difficult days.

Rest assured that as you focus your prayers on others, the God who sees and hears also sees you and your needs. Therefore, pray for those who are heralding the Gospel message, whether at home or abroad. Pray that they walk blamelessly before God and remain true to the call and to the cause.

Let us pray that all may come to a saving knowledge of Christ Jesus and accept him as Lord of their lives. Let us pray for our children. Pray for their safety, success, and salvation. There are innumerable persons and matters for whom and about which we can pray. Let us, therefore, go boldly to the Mercy Seat and to the Throne of Grace as we pray in the name of the Lord Jesus.

11.

Difficult Days of Uncertainty

Philippians 1:12-18

Within days, the life of one of my friends was drastically changed occasioned by a debilitating physical condition which necessitated frequent hospitalization. The condition left her physically impaired and totally dependent on others for her care. My friend was in the prime of her life. She had been a faithful follower of the Lord. As I spoke with her during one of my visits, she boldly testified saying, "With all the indignity that I have suffered ... I do not understand it, but, if my illness is going to bring glory to God, in one way or the other, then hallelujah!"

The church at Philippi was established on the Apostle Paul's second missionary journey. He laboured among the believers until they came to spiritual maturity. It was evident that Paul and the Philippian believers enjoyed a congenial relationship that transcended the prison walls in which Paul was held. To demonstrate their continued love and support of Paul, the believers sent him gifts through his ministry associates, who visited him periodically.

Paul was kept informed about the welfare and well-being of the believers through the reports he received from his ministry associates. It was through these reports that he learned that the believers were experiencing fierce opposition from external forces and from believers within the body who were constantly at odds with each other.

The believers longed for Paul to be released from prison and to return to be with them. His presence would have brought about a measure of comfort and stability. However, there was no telling when, or whether Paul would be released from prison, or whether the church would withstand the opposition. The believers, therefore, were practising their faith in a climate of uncertainty. In this context, Paul wrote the letter to the Philippians with one of the objectives being to encourage them to persevere in their faith despite the prevailing uncertainties, including the uncertainty surrounding his release.

Philippians 1:12-18 is the passage of focus for this chapter. The passage unfolds three primary matters of interest, the first being identifying and focusing on divine purpose in challenging situations.

Identifying Divine Purpose

In Philippians 1:12, Paul wrote, "Now I want you to know, brothers, that what has happened to me has really served to advance the Gospel." In this verse, Paul intentionally shifted the believers' focus from the negative circumstances of his imprisonment to the profitable purpose that may have escaped them. He spared no moment to call the believers' attention to the fact that his imprisonment served the purpose of spreading the Gospel of Christ Jesus in two strategic ways.

The Spread of the Gospel in the Prison

First, the Gospel message was being advanced throughout the prison as Paul interacted with the soldiers, guards, and other prisoners. As Paul explained in Philippians 1:13, "As a result, it has become clear throughout the whole palace guard and to everyone else that I am in chains for Christ."

Because of the proximal space that Paul shared with the guards, they became aware of his impeccable conduct. Something different would have been seen in this prisoner that they may not have seen in the others. Paul's Christlike conduct would have signalled to the soldiers that there was something out of the ordinary about this prisoner.

The reasons for Paul's imprisonment may have become a topic of conversation among the soldiers and among the prisoners as well. It may have come to light that he was imprisoned for preaching about Jesus. The soldiers and the prisoners may, therefore, have questioned among themselves the significance and relevance of this Jesus about whom Paul spoke and for whose cause Paul was imprisoned. They may have come to appreciate that there was something of invaluable worth about Paul's Jesus, of whom he spoke and for whom he was willing to risk his life.

Paul's Christlike posture and his response to his imprisonment made a vehemently loud sound in the ears of those with whom he shared space in the prison. Simply put, there is no stopping the accomplishment of the purpose of the Almighty God. Soldiers thought they were stymying the advancement of the Gospel when they imprisoned Paul. Imprisonment would have been a difficult experience for him, but God used that experience to advance the cause of the Gospel.

Empowerment of Other Believers

Philippians 1:14-18 reveals that Paul's imprisonment also served to spread the Gospel on an additional level.

> Because of my chains, most of the brothers in the Lord have been encouraged to speak the word of God more courageously and fearlessly. It is true that some preach Christ out of envy and rivalry, but others out of goodwill. The latter do so in love, knowing that I am put here for the defence of the Gospel. The former preach Christ out of selfish ambition, not sincerely, supposing that they can stir up trouble for me while I am in chains. But what does it matter?

It is believed that there was a body of Christian believers in Rome prior to Paul's arrival there. However, the socio-political climate in Rome might have been anti-Christianity. In this climate of hostility, some believers were fearful about sharing the Gospel due to the expectation of fierce opposition. However, knowing that Paul was in prison for the sake of the Gospel stirred a sense of fearlessness, confidence, and courage in the other believers, who then began to speak about Christ Jesus with increased boldness.

Reasons to Rejoice

Paul's protracted imprisonment occasioned the promulgation of the Gospel of Christ Jesus. He noted, however, that the motives of some of the preachers were incorrect. Interestingly, Paul was not fazed by this reality. His response was, "What does it matter? The important thing is that in every way, whether from false motives or true, Christ is preached. And because of this, I rejoice" (Philippians 1:18).

The picture here shows Paul assuming a posture of rejoicing amid much uncertainty and what may have been ill-conceived motives. He chose to look past the ills and see the positives and the possibilities. He was still in prison, was uncertain about the outcome, but the Gospel was being preached, and that was reason enough to rejoice.

Alongside the joy that resided in Paul's heart was the spirit of confidence that he exuded, as was evident in Philippians 1:19:

> For I know that through your prayers and the help given by the Spirit of Jesus Christ, what has happened to me will turn out for my deliverance. I eagerly expect and hope that I will in no way be ashamed, but will have sufficient courage so that now, as always Christ will be exalted in my body, whether by life or by death. For to me, to live is Christ and to die is gain.

Imprisonment could not have been a comfortable experience for Paul. He could have chosen to complain about the untenable circumstances. He could have spent the time crafting his defence and praying for his release. Instead, Paul assumed a posture of confidence and contentment and focused on the divine purpose of his being in prison.

Reasons to be Confident

Paul knew with unwavering certainty that, whatever the outcome of his imprisonment, he would be in a good place. He therefore said,

> "I eagerly expect and hope that I will in no way be ashamed, but will have sufficient courage so that now, as always Christ will be exalted in my body, whether by life or by death. For to me, to live is Christ and to die is gain. (Philippians 1:20-22)

The confident posture that Paul assumed during the difficult circumstances of his life was attributed to the prayers of the believers and the power of the Holy Spirit. He therefore said, "… I know that through your prayers and the help given by the Spirit of Jesus Christ, what has happened to me will turn out for my deliverance" (Philippians 1:19).

Paul's acknowledgement of the prayers of the believers and the help of the Holy Spirit is evidence that he recognized his limitations and the need for physical and spiritual support during the difficult circumstances of his life. He may have been overtaken by feelings of despondency and discouragement had he not been undergirded by the prayers of the believers and the power of the Holy Spirit throughout his challenging experience. Little wonder, therefore, that he remained joyful and confident amidst the prevailing challenges of the day.

Positioning to Stand Firm

There is no doubt that the times in which we live are difficult on every front. Our experiences sometimes leave us feeling battered and bruised. Oh, the joy of knowing that God causes all things to work together for our good and for God's eternal glory! (Romans 8:38). Amidst the pain of our difficult experiences, God has a purpose, and God's purpose will prevail. The prognosis may be bad, but God is still in control, and the purpose of the Sovereign God will be accomplished on the earth.

Our response to difficult situations is, in and of itself, a testimony of the God that we serve. In this vein, it is helpful to endeavour to see the good that may result from challenging situations. Admittedly, we cannot always see God's purpose in all our experiences. In these circumstances, it is in order to ask God to help us gain perspective and view the situation from His vantage point.

Seeing the good in seemingly difficult situations helps to produce joy in our hearts. Joy, which is the feeling of goodwill in spite of the circumstances, is a valuable commodity during challenging times. The joy of the Lord strengthens us (Nehemiah 8:10) and keeps us emotionally and spiritually grounded in our difficult days.

There is something to be said about the need for believers to be supported as they face the difficult days of their lives. It is deeply encouraging to know that we are not alone as we navigate a difficult patch. Let us commit to offering tangible and intangible support to a brother or a sister who is experiencing difficult days.

We may not be able to offer financial support, but we can pray. Although we may not be able to visit, we can bridge the distance with technology and connect with our brother and sister remotely. Whatever it takes, let us commit to supporting each other through the challenging days of uncertainties in which we now live, and so bring praise to the name of Jesus.

12.
Difficult Days of Disunity

Philippians 1:27-28; 4:1

It was with much joy that my sister and I listened to 89-year-old Sister Clarice (not her real name) as she shared with us several testimonies of the goodness of God to her over the 62 years of her walking with Him. She became a believer 32 years before her husband did. Being "unequally yoked" to an unbeliever resulted in difficult days of heart-wrenching trials for her. Notwithstanding, Sister Clarice was determined to stand firm in the faith and remain true to her Lord and Saviour in word and conduct.

Philippians 1:27-28 and 2:1-8 are the passages of focus in this chapter. The passages draw attention to the course of action that was prescribed to arrest the wave of disunity that plagued the Philippian church, resulting from internal factions and external forces.

Christ-Like Code of Conduct

The believers in Philippi calculated that if Paul were to be released from prison, he would visit with them and help to restore unity among the body. Since his release was uncertain, Paul sought to address the issue in the letter that he wrote to the church.

> Whatever happens, conduct yourselves in a manner worthy of the Gospel of Christ. Then, whether I come and see you or only hear about you in my absence, I will know that you stand firm in one spirit, contending as one man for the faith of the Gospel without being frightened in any way by those who oppose you. This is a sign to them that they will be destroyed, but that you will be saved—and that by God. (Philippians 1:27–28)

The verses begin with the general call for the believers to "conduct yourselves in a manner worthy of the Gospel of Christ." The statement raises the question of what constitutes conduct that is worthy of the gospel of Christ Jesus. The passage lists at least six essentials that should become the code of conduct for the believers: unity, fearlessness, love, selflessness, humility, and cheerfulness.

Unity

Clearly, there were matters about which the believers in Philippi disagreed. Their anxious hope was that Paul would have been released from prison, in which case he could have visited with them to help quieten the contrary winds of disunity that prevailed among them.

Since Paul was uncertain about the outcome of his imprisonment, he spared no moment to have the believers know that if they were going to withstand the external forces, it was imperative that they settle their differences and advance as a united force against their opponents. The call for unity among the believers was palpable and was repeated in Philippians 2:2—"make my joy complete by being like-minded, having the same love, being one in spirit and of one mind."

Disunity is disturbing and destructive. Disunity creates the entrance through which the enemy can infiltrate the camp and disintegrate the fellowship. Disunity is misrepresentative of the Body of Christ and should be eliminated. A united body of believers is better able to withstand the disruptive forces of evil. The life of the church pivots on the fulcrum of unity, and it must be preserved at all costs.

Fearlessness

Fearlessness is another of the essentials of conduct that is worthy of the Gospel of Christ. The encouragement to the believers, therefore, was that they should live "... without being frightened in any way by those who oppose you. This is a sign to them that they will be destroyed, but that you will be saved—and that by God." (Philippians 1:28).

The opposition was fierce and furious; it was caustic and well calculated. However, the believers should not allow themselves to demonstrate even a modicum of fear in the face of their opponents. Instead, they should be careful to face their opponents with an abundance of courage and boldness. This posture would serve as a testimony of the empowering and enabling grace of Christ Jesus, their Lord.

Love

The believers were encouraged to practise love as becoming conduct that was "worthy of the Gospel of Christ."

> If you have any encouragement from being united with Christ, if any comfort from his love, if any fellowship with the Spirit, if any tenderness and compassion, then make my joy complete by being like-minded, having

the same love, being one in spirit and purpose. (Philippians 2:1-2)

The reference to the love of Christ is significant. The indication is that disunity will be dispelled where love of the similitude of Christ's love for the believers is practised. In summary, Christ's love for the believers was sacrificial. He offered His life as the penalty for the believers' sin. That was the ultimate sacrifice! The call, therefore, was for the believers to love each other sacrificially, to the extent that they give up their rights for the sake of unity. That is the extent of love that becomes "worthy of the Gospel of Christ", and that would dispel disunity among the body of believers.

Selflessness

Conduct that is "worthy of the Gospel of Christ" is also characterized by selflessness. Philippians 2:3-4 implored the believers to "do nothing out of selfish ambition or vain conceit, but in humility value others above yourselves. Each of you should look not to your own interests, but also to the interests of others."

It is fair to say that self-interest is at the centre of disunity. Advancing the interests of the other believers is the antidote for disunity. That is precisely what the Christ of the Christian faith did. He forsook His own interest for the sake of the believers. Likewise, believers are called to forsake their own interests for the interests of each other. Where this becomes the common practice, then the interests of everyone will be served. In this context, the picture of unity will be clearly displayed and will serve as a solid testimony to those who stoutly oppose the faith.

Humility

The call for demonstrations of humility is issued alongside the call for selflessness, indicating that both practices are closely aligned. The alignment is clearly reflected in Philippians 2:3: "Do nothing out of selfish ambition or vain conceit. Rather, in humility value others above yourselves, not looking to your own interests but each of you to the interests of the others."

It takes humility of spirit to be able to "value others above self," and to prioritize the "interests of others" above your own interests. But that is the conduct that is becoming of the Gospel of Christ Jesus. That is the conduct that dispels disunity and disarms the opposers of the faith.

Cheerfulness

The climate of disunity is characterized by drudgery and cheerlessness. Therefore, it can be appreciated that cheerfulness must also be included among the essentials that bespeak conduct that is worthy of the Gospel of Christ. In the words of Philippians 2:14-16, the Philippians were encouraged to "do everything without complaining or arguing, so that you may become blameless and pure, children of God without fault in a crooked and depraved generation."

The spirit of cheerfulness is attractive to the onlooker. It becomes a witness to the onlooker of the grace of God in the lives of those who serve Him. Little wonder, then, that, with the spirit of cheerfulness, the believers will "… shine among them like stars in the sky as you hold firmly to the word of life." Quite a compelling witness!

Christ: The Standard Bearer

Paul summarised his exhortation on conduct that is worthy of the Gospel of Christ in Philippians 2:5-8, which points the believers to Christ Himself as the standard bearer.

> Your attitude should be the same as that of Christ Jesus. Who, being in very nature God, did not consider equality with God something to be grasped, But made himself nothing, taking the very nature of a servant, being made in human likeness. And being

found in appearance as a man, he humbled himself by becoming obedient to death— even death on a cross!

The Christian conduct that Paul advocated and expected to be demonstrated by believers was exemplified by Jesus for the sake of reuniting believers with God. In this vein, it should not be onerous for the believers to endeavour to foster the spirit of unity within the body.

By virtue of his imprisonment, Paul could not have been physically present among the believers during the difficult days of disunity. He could not have helped them settle their differences, nor could he stave off the attacks of the opponents. However, his heart's desire for the believers was that they stand firm in the faith in all circumstances.

Having comprehensively explicated the essentials of "conduct worthy of the Gospel of Christ", and having held up Christ Jesus as the standard bearer of the code of conduct, Paul then concluded his exhortation with the words of Philippians 4:1, "Therefore, my brothers, you whom I love and long for, my joy and crown, stand firm in the Lord, dear friends!"

Positioning to Stand Firm

How well do you behave during your difficult experiences? Would the way you conduct yourself during your difficult experiences reflect the life and beauty of Jesus? Regardless of your circumstances, the call is for you to ensure that your behaviour always exemplifies Christian conduct.

The standards of conduct that the Philippian believers were encouraged to adopt and practice during their difficult days should also be the hallmark of the conduct of believers in this age: unity, fearlessness, love, selflessness, humility, and cheerfulness.

Disunity is a lethal weapon of the enemy of the body of Christ. Little wonder, therefore, that there are so many "break-away brands" of the faith. It is the inconsequential things that tend to bring about disunity within the Christian community. Instead of focusing on the real adversary, believers sometimes turn inward and destroy each other.

Believers are encouraged to dispense with suspicion, cynicism, impatience, intolerance, unkind criticisms, and unpleasant remarks about each other. These practices foster and facilitate disunity. Better, therefore, to cement interpersonal relationships with the "bond of peace" (Ephesians 4:3) and advance the welfare and well-being of each other.

Unity makes room for tenacity both on the individual and collective levels. The believer who is buckling under the pressure of their difficult experience will be strengthened by the support offered by the other believers. The body of believers, as a collective, will better withstand opposition when there is unity. It is possible to remain faithful to the cause during difficult days of opposition, as believers resolve to stand in unity and bring praise to the name of Jesus, their Saviour and Lord.

13.

Difficult Days of Anxiety

Philippians 4:6-7

According to the American Psychological Association, (n.d.), "Anxiety is an emotion characterized by feelings of tension, worried thoughts, and physical changes like increased blood pressure." Considering these debilitating effects of anxiety, this emotion should be identified for what it is, and efforts should be made to prevent it from becoming a part of our lived experience.

The Apostle Paul recognized that the believers in Philippi were overcome by anxiety. Therefore, he concluded his letter to the church by addressing the issue and presenting the believers with the antidote for anxiety. Philippians 4:6-7 is the passage of focus in this chapter, which calls attention to three matters of interest, the first being the indications of anxiety.

Indications of Anxiety

Due to the prevailing circumstances, a wave of anxiety had engulfed the believers in the church at Philippi. They were surrounded by persons who stoutly opposed the faith. That reality was a breeding ground for anxiety about their safety. To compound the issue, some of the believers were swayed by selfish motives, a reality that threatened the unity and stability of the church and generated levels of anxiety. The uncertainty of Paul's release from prison was also a source of anxiety for the believers.

In Philippians 4:6, Paul captured the believers' attention with the compelling statement, "Do not be anxious about anything ..." This statement succinctly suggests that Paul was aware that the believers were overcome by anxiety. The Apostle, therefore, presented the believers with a prescription for anxiety; the second matter of interest in this chapter.

The Prescription for Anxiety

Philippians 4:6b continued with the words, "... but in every situation, by prayer and petition, with thanksgiving, present your request to God." There is something jolting about the word "but" that moves the believers' attention away from what preceded it to the contrasting point.

In this context, Paul seemed to pull the believers' attention away from the place of futility to the place of possibility and prosperity. It is in this space that he then prescribed prayer as the remedy for anxiety. Since prayer is considered a remedy for anxiety, it should be closely examined for its worth. In this vein, three observations are made about prayer.

Prayer Connects the Believer with God

Through prayer, the believer establishes connectivity with the Almighty God and the eternal resources of heaven. Prayer is simply talking with God. "Prayer is the offering up of our desires to God, or making them known to him" (Matthew Henry, Nov. 10, 2025, para 8). God hears and answers the prayers of those who come to Him.

Prayer as a Constant Way of Life

To pray "... in every situation" suggests that this practice makes room for the believer to adopt a posture of prayer as a way of life. If things are going well, share that with God; talk to him about it. If things are awry, talk to God about that as well. "We must not only keep up stated times for prayer, but we must pray upon every particular emergency ..." (Matthew Henry, Nov. 10, 2015, para. 9). The believer has the privilege of always presenting every conceivable matter to God. No anxiety-inducing issue is too large or too small to be brought to God's attention.

Prayer Takes Various Forms

The instruction "… by prayer and petition, with thanksgiving, present your request to God" points the believers to the variety of ways in which they converse with God. Prayer is the general act of simply conversing with God. It bespeaks the pivotal communication that defines the relationship that God has with believers. However, "A petition, just as it is in the political arena, is a request to a sovereign to take some action. Any request made of God [for help or guidance], is thus a petition" (Matthew Henry, Nov. 10, 2015, para. 3).

Prayers should also take the form of thanksgiving— expressions of gratitude to God for the many ways in which He favours His children. "We must not only seek supplies of good, but own receipts of mercy. Grateful acknowledgements of what we have, argue a right disposition of mind and are prevailing motives for further blessings" (Matthew Henry, 2015, para. 8). Against this backdrop, believers do well to pray about the presenting issues rather than become anxious about them.

Prescriptions are intended to bring about the desired and expected results. In this vein, prayer has been shown to be a prescription that has transformative results for believers who are overtaken by anxiety. The result of a prayerful approach to presenting difficulties becomes the third matter of interest.

Results of a Prayerful Lifestyle

In Philippians 4:7, the believers were informed that in adopting a prayerful approach to their troubles, "… the peace of God, which transcends all understanding, will guard your hearts and your minds in Christ Jesus." In this context, the "peace of God" points to "the comfortable sense of our reconciliation to God and interest in His favour, and the hope of the heavenly blessedness, and enjoyment of God hereafter …" (Matthew Henry, Nov. 10, 2015, para 8). The peace that God gives to believers who unburden their souls before Him results in an all-encompassing state of physical, emotional and spiritual wholeness and well-being that no other source allows.

Being reconciled with God brings the believer into a wholesome father-and-child relationship. This relationship brings with it the unwavering confidence that the all-knowing, all-powerful, ever-present God will sufficiently address the assailing matters. In this relationship, the believer is at ease in committing everything to God. Prayer, therefore, is an exchange in which believers give their burdens to God and He, in turn, gives them His peace. There is no room for anxiety in a peaceful environment.

Philippians 4:7 succinctly distinguishes the peace that comes from God from the peace that comes from other sources. Simply put, the peace that comes from God surpasses human comprehension. In that sense, peace that comes from God cannot be compared with peace that comes from alternative sources.

The peace that comes from the God of endless resources is inexhaustible. The peace that comes from the God who is unfathomable is indescribable. The peace that comes from the infinite God is indestructible. "This peace will keep our hearts and minds through Christ Jesus; it will keep us from sinning under our troubles, and from sinking under them; keep us calm and sedate, without discomposure of passion, and with inward satisfaction" (Matthew Henry Bible Commentary, 2015, para. 9). There is nothing like the peace of God!

Undoubtedly, the believers in Philippi did well if they demonstrated trust in God's ability to help them by assuming the posture of prayer in every situation. If anxiety suggests distrust in God's ability, then the posture of prayer signals trust in God's ability to provide the needed solution to the troubling matters.

Positioning to Stand Firm

It is easy to become anxious for the things relative to life and living: the unpaid mortgage that may result in the loss of your property; the outcome of the job interview which will determine whether you are given the job; the performance evaluation that will determine whether you are promoted on the job; the overdue school fee, which will determine whether you continue in the programme of study; the outcome of the surgery, which will determine whether you live or die.

Anxiety suggests that we distrust God's ability to help us. It also suggests reliance on oneself to find solutions for the presenting issues. The reality, however, is that anxiety is generated from our repeated failed attempts to fix the problems. There are some issues that are completely outside our scope and sphere of influence; we simply cannot fix them.

The same is true about the individuals who cause us anxious moments. We cannot fix them. At the same time, there may be aspects of ourselves that we struggle to change. For all the anxiety-producing matters, the peace of God is the solution. The transformative practice, therefore, is to bring all the anxiety-producing matters to God in prayer.

To which believer does anxiety bring solutions? No one! What solutions does anxiety bring to the presenting issues?

None! There is nothing to gain from being anxious. Anxiety does not provide solutions and answers. Anxiety complicates the situation where the anxious person experiences physical impairments for which remedial attention must be given.

It is helpful to know that every discipline is anchored in the knowledge and wisdom of the Almighty God. In this vein, believers should not hesitate to engage the services of qualified and trusted practitioners for help to overcome anxiety-producing issues.

Above all, believers are well-advised to develop the art of engaging in a two-way conversation with God and listening to, and doing what He says, whether in spoken or written words. This is the single most tested and tried solution for the difficult days of anxiety.

14.

Embracing Difficult Days

2 Corinthians 11:23-29; Philippians 1:29-30; 1 Peter 4:1-16

The day following my water baptism, one of my Grade 3 classmates started hitting me for no apparent reason. I was never one to fight back. I walked away from her, but she followed me around the school yard, calling me "Christian" and "long frock" as she continued to hit me on the back. What for? To this day, I have no idea except to say I was suffering for the sake of my faith.

This chapter calls into focus 2 Corinthians 11:23-29; 1 Peter 4:1, 12-16; and Philippians 1:29. The passages highlight three matters of interest, the first being the diverse nature of suffering.

The Diverse Nature of Suffering

In 2 Corinthians 11:23-29, Paul described the experience he had while ministering in Asia. He spoke of the five times in which he received 39 lashes, how he was once stoned, the time when he suffered shipwreck, the several storms he encountered as he travelled by sea from one place to the other, his being persecuted by his fellow Jews as well as by foreigners on several occasions, and the false accusations by the believers. Paul also spoke of weariness and painfulness, hunger and thirst, cold and nakedness, and the pain of attending to the needs of the believers.

A close examination of the suffering that Paul endured reveals that it varied in nature, encompassing a range of physical, social, emotional, mental, and spiritual circumstances. Paul's experiences also reveal that suffering originates from various sources, including within the community of believers.

Regardless of the nature and source of suffering, it has the propensity to cause ill-prepared and unsupported believers to falter or, at worst, abandon the faith. It is with this awareness that believers should prepare themselves for suffering. The letter to the Philippians had much to say to the believers in this regard.

The Mark of the Christian Faith

Philippians 1:29 unequivocally states, "For it has been granted to you on behalf of Christ not only to believe on him, but also to suffer for him, ... " The New Bible Commentary (1970) informs that, "The verb *granted* conveys the thought of a gift of grace: to you has the privilege been freely given" (p. 1954). The gift of salvation is "granted", given to the believer by the grace of God. In the same vein, suffering is "granted" (given) to the believer as a gift from God by His grace.

The word "also" connects the grace of believing with the grace of suffering. Believing and suffering are intricately interwoven. Those who believe and receive Christ Jesus also receive His suffering, which is construed to be the indelible symbol of the faith; the mark of identification that those who embrace the faith belong to the company of Jesus and his saints throughout the ages. No wonder Paul rejoiced in his suffering and encouraged the Philippian believers to do the same.

The Common Experience

Philippians 1:30 continued to help the believers in Philippi come to terms with the suffering they were experiencing at the hands of those who stoutly opposed the faith. "You are going through the same struggle you saw I had, and now hear that I still have." The word "struggle" suggests hardship that occasions "blood, sweat, and tears" and fittingly describes the experience of the believers as they contend for the faith and take a stand for right living.

To put the "struggle" in context, Paul pointed the believers to his own struggles, those he experienced in the past, and those that he was still experiencing at the time of his writing. The believers were all too familiar with the sufferings that Paul endured. They, themselves, had supported him in his struggles.

In that context, Paul was helping the believers in Philippi to come to terms with the fact that suffering is a common experience shared by all believers. The nature and source of suffering may differ, but it is the common cause of Christ for which they all suffer. The believers could, therefore, embrace their suffering and take comfort in knowing that they were in the company of innumerable believers.

The Apostle Peter underscored the fact of the commonality of suffering in his letter to the believers in Rome. To encourage the believers, he addressed them as friends and said, "… do not be surprised at the painful trial you are suffering, as though something strange were happening to you" (1 Peter 4:12). As it were, the believers should understand that what they were experiencing was what other believers were also experiencing.

Reasons to Rejoice

The Apostle Peter admitted that the believers' experiences were painful. In the same breath, he carefully highlighted two salient reasons for them to rejoice, inasmuch as they are suffering. In the first place, the believers should "...rejoice inasmuch as you participate in the sufferings of Christ, so that you may be overjoyed when his glory is revealed" (1 Peter 4:13). Suffering for the sake of the name of Jesus is quite an indescribable badge of honour for which believers should rejoice.

1 Peter 4:14 identifies a second reason for those who suffer for the name of Jesus to rejoice: "If you are insulted because of the name of Christ, you are blessed, for the Spirit of glory and of God rests on you." Suffering for the sake of the name of Jesus is associated with an unsurpassable blessing, which gives the believers very good reason to rejoice.

Positioning to Stand Firm

As a believer in Christ Jesus, it is essential that you acknowledge the reality that suffering is the hallmark of the Christian faith. Believers will, therefore, suffer on account of their faith in one way or another. Suffering on account of the faith arises, for example, when believers face opposition as they proclaim the message of salvation. Suffering on account of the faith presents when believers are marginalised in the workplace or the community, as they take a stand for right living. Believers may even be put to death for the sake of the Gospel of Christ Jesus.

God forbid that believers should buckle under the pressure of their difficult circumstances and begin to question the veracity of the faith, the goodness of God, the care of the Lord, and the sense in continuing to believe in Christ Jesus. Believers are more likely to persevere and stand firm in their faith during difficult days of suffering if they remember that suffering is an integral part of the Christian faith. It is the hallmark of the faith; the testimony that they are on the Lord's side; that they are soldiers of the cross of Jesus; that they are in the struggle for the cause of Christ.

If you are a believer and have not yet faced challenges, you can expect that the day will come when your faith will be tested and tried in one way or another. When your difficult days come, remember that you are not alone in the struggle for the cause of Christ. Believers of past ages suffered for the name of Christ Jesus. Believers in this present age are suffering for the name of Jesus. Believers in the ages to come will also suffer for the name of Christ Jesus.

Rejoice to know that you are in the privileged company of others who have experienced suffering, or who are suffering for the cause of Christ Jesus. Comfort yourself in knowing that the Spirit of God rests upon you, and rejoice in your suffering

Some believers have died in the struggle, but they held fast to their faith. You, too, should "arm yourself with the same attitude" of suffering (1 Peter 4:1) and remain steadfast in the faith during your difficult days.

15.

Difficult Days of Death

Acts6:5-18

In May 2024, a 23-year-old missionary and his 21-year-old wife of two years were ambushed and savagely murdered while on an overseas missionary assignment. They knew that the country in which they were to serve was overrun by dissident citizens. They knew that their lives would have been imperilled. But they were committed to Christ Jesus and the cause for which they died.

Difficult days sometimes end in death—it did for one believer in the early Church. The posture that he assumed in the face of death is the focus of the reflections in this chapter. Acts Chapter 6 provides an account of the exponential numerical growth of the early Church as people came to believe and accept the Gospel message. Due to the increasing number of believers, it became necessary for the Church to elect qualified men who would be primarily responsible for attending to the welfare needs of the members while the apostles continued to devote themselves to prayer and the delivery of the Word of God.

Stephen was one of seven "qualified" men (deacons) who were elected to address the welfare needs of the believers. Acts 6:5-9 was careful to record that Stephen was "a man full of faith and of the Holy Spirit ... a man full of God's grace and power." There are three observations made about Stephen that contextualize the difficult days that he experienced as he fulfilled his role as a deacon in the Church. The first observation is his passion for the work of the Lord despite the opposition that he encountered.

Passion Despite Opposition

According to Acts 6:10, "Stephen, a man full of God's grace and power, did great wonders and miraculous signs among the people." It is likely that Stephen's "social welfare" work among the community of believers included ensuring that everyone was adequately fed, that those who were ill were visited and treated, that emotional needs were addressed, and that relationships were repaired and restored. Despite the extensive work done among the people, some individuals openly and fiercely opposed Stephen and his ministry.

According to Acts 6:9-14,

> Opposition arose … from members of the Synagogue of the Freedmen. These men began to argue with Stephen, but they could not stand up against his wisdom or the Spirit by whom he spoke. Then they secretly persuaded some men to say, "We have heard Stephen speak words of blasphemy against Moses and against God." So … they stirred up the people and the elders, and the teachers of the law. produced false witnesses … they seized Stephen and brought him before the Sanhedrin.

The ruler of the Sanhedrin, the ancient Jewish court system (Schoenberg, n.d., para. 1), asked Stephen to defend himself against his accusers. However, Stephen had no such interest or intention! He was more interested in and intent on doing the work to which he was assigned and defending the Gospel of Christ Jesus.

In response to the High Priest, Stephen seized the moment to launch into a sermon that charted Israel's history, beginning with Abraham, and ending with the crucified Christ. The rulers of the Sanhedrin did not countenance Stephen's sermon. "When they heard this [Stephen's sermon], they were furious and gnashed their teeth at him" (Acts 7:54). But Stephen remained undaunted and persevered to the end. This becomes the second observation made.

Persevering to the End

The intent of the mob was to stone Stephen to death. Throughout this difficult ordeal, Stephen kept his gaze fixed on heaven—not on his adversaries—and assumed a posture of prayer as the stones came bearing down on his body with one threatening blow after the other. "While they were stoning him, Stephen prayed, 'Lord Jesus, receive my spirit.' Then he fell on his knees and cried out, 'Lord, do not hold this sin against them.' When he had said this, he fell asleep" (Acts 7:60).

Close examination of the content of Stephen's prayer reveals that he was not asking to be delivered from impending death. Stephen was prepared and ready to die for the cause of Christ. Therefore, he positioned himself to die and only asked God to receive his spirit.

Further examination of the prayer reveals that Stephen was also praying for forgiveness for those who were hurling stones at him. This prayer of forgiveness was clear evidence that Stephen himself had forgiven his adversaries. What an admirable display of courage in the face of death!

The Presence of God

The posture of prayer that Stephen assumed and the spirit of courage that he demonstrated in the face of death are attributable to the empowering and enabling power of the Holy Spirit. According to Acts 7:55-60,

> Stephen, full of the Holy Spirit, looked up to heaven and saw the glory of God, and Jesus standing at the right hand of God. "Look!" he said, "I see heaven open and the Son of man standing at the right hand of God."

The picture painted in Acts 7:55-60 is that Stephen was not alone in his final moments of life. All of heaven was there with him as he drew his final breath. No wonder, then, that he faced death with courage and confidence and without fear or compromise of his faith.

God was not delivering Stephen from the hand of his accusers, but He was there watching over His servant. God was not heard to say anything as death closed in on Stephen, but He was there, fuelling and sustaining him with strength and courage to face death. Stephen did not have to face death alone, for the God about whom he preached was very much there at the time of his death!

Positioning to Stand Firm

Suffering for the name and cause of Christ Jesus may result in death. Countless believers have died and are dying for the cause of Christ Jesus. Death, in these circumstances, is not a sign of defeat. It is a sign of triumph and faithfulness to God. How prepared are you to face death?

The fear of death is triggered by the understandable fear of the unknown. The believer does well to be guided by what the Bible teaches about death and life after death. Eternal life is promised to every believer, as stated in John 3:16. Jesus prepared His disciples for His death, burial, and resurrection when He said,

> In my Father's house are many rooms; if it were not so, I would have told you. If it were not so, I would have told you. I am going there to prepare a place for you. And if I go and prepare a place for you, I will come back and take you to be with me, that you also may be where I am (John 14:2-3).

The believer also does well to remember that, by His own death on the cross, Jesus conquered death. 1 Corinthians 15:55-56 are words of comfort for Christ's followers:

Where, O death, is your victory? Where, O death, is your sting? The sting of death is sin, and the power of sin is the law. But thanks be to God! He gives us the victory through our Lord Jesus Christ.

There is no need to fear death and dying, for God will be there with the believer at the time of death. David had that assurance and therefore wrote in Psalm 23:4, "Even though I walk through the darkest valley, I will fear no evil, for you are with me; your rod and your staff, they comfort me." May believers come to know that even in death, our faithful God is with us, and we can face this final enemy as courageous soldiers of the cross of Christ Jesus.

PART II
Sources of Support

16.

Comfort from God

2nd Corinthians 1:1-11

My friend who resides overseas was forced to return home to attend to the needs of her family. Her sister who cared for their ailing mother, suffered a debilitating physical ailment that prevented her from continuing in the assigned role. In several ways, it was a difficult experience for my friend and her family. I listened attentively as she expressed gratitude for the support she received from her friends during those difficult days. She concluded that the worst thing is to experience aloneness when faced with challenging situations.

The passage of focus in this chapter is 2 Corinthians 1:1-11. It recounts the challenges that Paul and his ministry associates encountered for the sake of the Gospel of Christ Jesus and the help that they received from God.

The God of Comfort

Paul began his second letter to the Corinthians with an eruption of praise to God for the support He offered to him and his ministry associates during their challenging experiences.

> Praise be to the God and Father of our Lord Jesus Christ, the Father of compassion and the God of all comfort, who comforts us in all our troubles, so that we can comfort those in any trouble with the comfort we ourselves have received from God. (2 Corinthians 1:1-7)

Paul's reference to God as "the Father of compassion" and the "God of all comfort" is insightful. The suggestion is that the troubles that he and his associates experienced necessitated compassion and comfort. The gravity of the challenges the men experienced is summarized in 2 Corinthians 1:8-9 and aids our appreciation of their need for compassion and comfort.

> We do not want you to be uninformed, brothers, about the hardships we suffered in the province of Asia. We were under great pressure, far beyond our ability to endure, so that we despaired even of life. Indeed, in our hearts we felt the sentence of death. But this happened that we might not rely on ourselves but on God, who raises the dead.

The terminologies that Paul used to describe the challenges he and his associates faced suggest that these were the worst possible experiences: "great pressure", "far beyond our ability to endure", "we despaired of life", and "we felt the sentence of death." Neither their education nor their expertise could have helped them in those difficult circumstances. Seemingly, they would have succumbed to despair and depression were it not for the intervention of the "Father of compassion" and the "God of all comfort."

The comfort of God speaks to encouragement for the heart and mind, a lifting of the spirit when it is cast down, and the restoration of a wounded soul. The comfort of God varies in nature and is need-specific. Essentially, the comfort of God enables and empowers the believer to endure suffering and persevere to the end.

To Paul and his ministry associates, God's comfort was life-giving and preserving. It was transformative and restorative. God's comfort was like ointment to physical, emotional, and spiritual wounds. In all the trouble that Paul and his associates encountered, God was there with them and, out of an abundance of compassion, had given them all the support they needed to successfully navigate their challenging experiences. No wonder, then, that the ministers could stand firm in the faith and persevere through the sufferings with hearts of thanksgiving.

The Faithfulness of God

With reference to the support that Paul received from the Father of compassion and the God of all comfort, he said, "He has delivered us from such a deadly peril, and He will deliver us again. On Him we have set our hope that He will continue to deliver us, ..." (2 Corinthians 1:10).

For good reason, Paul and his associates would probably again face the threat of death as they continued to preach the Gospel of Jesus Christ. He admitted in 2 Corinthians 1:9 that, "... this happened that we might not rely on ourselves but on God, who raises the dead." The difficult experiences served as a constant reminder that the work in which the men were engaged was all about God. It was His work, His church, and His people.

The challenges kept Paul and his associates in prayer to the God of the ministry. They needed to rely on him for all the needed resources and for help in times of trouble. Based on God's deliverance in the difficult experiences of the past, Paul and his ministry associates could face the future with confidence that He would deliver them again. They would not need to fear, for the One who raises the dead is a faithful, dependable, and trustworthy God, and He would continue to deliver them.

People as Agents of Support

Paul was confident of God's help in times of trouble. However, 2 Corinthians 1:10b and 11 indicate that he was also aware of the believers' invaluable role as instruments through whom God would provide the extent of the help that was needed. On that basis, Paul wrote, "On him we have set our hope that He will continue to deliver us, as you help us by your prayers."

The phrase "as you help us by your prayers" links God's deliverance with the prayers of the believers. In effect, the believers themselves were invaluable instruments through whom God supported Paul and his ministry associates. The believers could not have accompanied Paul like his associates in the ministry, but they could pray. Some of them may not have been able to provide him with material support, but they could pray to the God of resources. The prayer of the believers was an essential component of the support that Paul needed and received from God.

It was important for Paul to show the believers the connection between their prayers and the help that he and his ministry associates received from God. They were, in effect, pivotal instruments in God's hands. Through their prayers, they were partnering with God to execute His work on the earth. In this vein, 2 Corinthians 1:11 ends with the statement, "Then many will give thanks on our behalf for the gracious favor granted us in answer to the prayers of many." The praying believers, God's invaluable instruments in providing support, would later be able to join in thanksgiving to God for the deliverance and the success of the ministry.

Positioning to Stand Firm

It is not unusual for believers to ask, "Why does God allow bad things to happen to good people?" Know, though, that trials serve to teach us to depend on God and not on our own strength and abilities. It is easy for us to become self-reliant and act independently of God. Of course, there is little, if anything, to gain from that attitude and approach. We do well to remember that of ourselves we can do nothing, for our sufficiency is of God (2 Corinthians 3:5).

The difficult situation that you are currently experiencing qualifies you to receive and be supported by the comfort that only God can give. Expect Him to comfort and carry you through that situation. The Holy Bible, God's written Word, is replete with words of comfort. Ask the Holy Spirit to guide you to the scripture that is specific to your situation. Also, ask Him to use the written Word to quieten your spirit and comfort your heart.

Like David, believers should also practise the principle of comforting themselves. Use the "voice" of the natural world that your God created to comfort yourself in your difficult situation. Remind yourself that the God who appoints the sun to stay in its course is the God who is with you in your difficult situation. The God who causes the leaves to change their colour in one season and the next is the same God who journeys with you, and will carry, comfort, and sustain you in your difficult experience.

17.

The Help of the Holy Spirit

Acts 3:11-26; 4:1-13

Mami T. was one to always offer words of encouragement to those with whom she spoke. One of her favourite expressions was, "Be of good cheer." Although Mami T. was the encourager par excellence, it became clear to me that she expected to be equally encouraged whenever she experienced difficulties. I once silently listened to Mami T as she shared with me the challenges that she was experiencing as she navigated the difficult days of old age. Toward the end of the narration, she paused and said, "And you would not even say, be of good cheer."

Words of comfort are medicine to the spirit of believers as they encounter difficult days. Acts 3:11-26 and Acts 4:1-13 are the passages of focus for this chapter, which examines the help that believers receive from the Holy Spirit during their difficult days. Acts 3:11-26 reports on the healing of a crippled man as Peter and John ministered to him, and the acrimonious response of the crowd that witnessed the healing. A summary of the story sets the stage for the focus on the support that believers receive from the Holy Spirit during difficult days.

According to the account given, those who witnessed the miracle in which the crippled man was healed ran towards Peter and John with great astonishment. The Apostles seized the opportunity to explain to the people that the man had been healed only in the name of Jesus, whom they had crucified but whom God had raised from the dead.

The people positively received the Apostles' message against the background of the miracle that was performed, so much so that "... many who heard the message believed, and the number of men grew to about five thousand" (Acts 4:4). The indisputable miracle and the positive response of the people infuriated the religious rulers. According to Acts 4:1-3,

> The priests and the captain of the temple guard and the Sadducees came up to Peter and John while they were speaking to the people. They were greatly disturbed because the apostles were teaching the people and proclaiming in Jesus the resurrection of the dead. They seized Peter and John and,

because it was evening, they put them in jail
until the next day.

Despite the time lapse, the city officials were no less irate the following day. Consequently, "The next day the rulers, elders and teachers of the law met in Jerusalem ... had Peter and John brought before them and began to question them: 'By what power or what name did you do this?'" (Acts 4:5).

It is apparent that the question was asked on intensely contentious grounds. The intent was to find a reason to incriminate and imprison Peter and John. Notwithstanding, they would not be outdone because they had the full support of the Holy Spirit during this acrimonious setting.

Empowered by the Holy Spirit

According to Acts 4:8-12, the boldness that only the Holy Spirit gives was on full display in Peter's response to the city officials:

> Then Peter, filled with the Holy Spirit, said to
> them: 'Rulers and elders of the people, if we
> are being called to account for an act of
> kindness shown to a cripple and are asked
> how he was healed, then, know this ... It is
> by the name of Jesus Christ of Nazareth,

whom you crucified but whom God raised from the dead, that this man stands before you healed. ... Salvation is found in no one else, for there is no other name under heaven given to men by which we must be saved.

Peter knew that his response would have further embroiled those who had asked the question of authority, but he spoke anyhow. What he had to say was antithetical to the belief of his listeners, but he simply seized the moment to declare the message of salvation through belief in Christ Jesus, albeit in an unfavourable environment.

The boldness with which Peter spoke was nothing short of the enabling of the Holy Spirit. According to Acts 4:13, "When they [the priests, the temple guards, and the Sadducees] saw the courage of Peter and John and realized that they were unschooled, ordinary men, they were astonished, and they took note that they had been with Jesus."

As the officials observed, there was something extraordinary about Peter and John. They were ordinary men, but they had spent three years with Jesus. That experience had radically changed their lives. Of course, they were ordinary men, but they had witnessed the resurrection of Jesus, who had been crucified and buried. That experience further transformed their lives. Peter and John were ordinary men, but they had been filled with the Holy Spirit, and He changed their lives from ordinary to extraordinary.

The Holy Spirit gave the Apostles the extraordinary courage and boldness they needed as they went about the business of heralding the good news of the Gospel of Jesus in a hostile environment. The Holy Spirit, most certainly, does extraordinary things with ordinary people! No wonder, therefore, that the contenders marvelled at the courage and boldness of the supposedly ordinary disciples.

"Courage is not the absence of fear but rather the willingness to act in obedience to God's calling and purposes, relying on His strength and guidance" (Wylie, 2023, para 1). Of themselves, the unlearned men, Peter and John, would have been crippled by fear as they stood before their learned opponents. However, by the power of the Holy Spirit, they had the courage to tell those who were well-versed in the written word of the day that salvation comes only through Jesus, the Living Word. By the power of the Holy Spirit, those two unschooled men had the courage to confound the no-resurrection theory of the Sadducees with their witness of the resurrection of Jesus by the power of the Holy Spirit.

Peter and John were not intimidated by the fact that the priests were authorities about matters of the law. There was no cowering simply because the Sadducees were more learned than the disciples were. The courage and boldness of the Holy Spirit enabled the men to stand up and to speak up despite the academic stature of those who stood before them.

Positioning to Stand Firm

Do you have the courage to take a stand for righteousness in the face of contention and intimidation? In these circumstances, ask the Holy Spirit to fill you with courage and boldness to get up and speak out.

Our post-modern world presents a plethora of philosophies and ideologies that run counter to the Gospel message. It will require the Holy Spirit to fill us with courage and boldness to publicly declare that only Jesus can transform the lives of both the learned and the unlearned. Only as the Holy Spirit fills us with extraordinary courage and boldness will we be able to challenge questionable political ideologies and stand as vanguards of right living in a world that is overtaken by unrighteousness.

Courage and boldness from the Holy Spirit elevate the believer from the ordinary to the extraordinary, eliminate fear, and enable the believer to declare that Jesus Christ is Lord, in the face of opposition and intimidation. Believers do well to remember that the Holy Spirit lives within us (John 14:16, 17) and stands ready to empower and enable us in every situation.

The need may not always be for courage and boldness. It may be for wisdom to make the right decision. It may be for peace in unsettling environments or joy in situations of despair. Whatever the need, the Holy Spirit is the believer's enabling and empowering Agent. We should, therefore, acknowledge the Holy Spirit's presence and appropriate His ability to help us navigate our challenging experiences.

18.
Collegial Support

Philippians 1:1, 2:19-24; 2 Timothy 4:9-13

Pastor Mark (not his real name) stood confidently at the podium to share his testimony about his call to pastoral ministry and snippets of his sojourn over the years. The occasion was his ordination service, and he seized the moment to acknowledge the extent of support that he enjoyed from his wife of several years. As Pastor Mark ended his response, he asked his wife to stand, much to the delight of the congregants, who then gave a thunderous round of applause.

The reflections in this chapter are grounded in Philippians 1:1, 2:19-24, and 2 Timothy 4:9-13. The passages highlight the extent to which the support that the Apostle Paul received from his colleagues in ministry helped him to navigate the difficulties that became his lived experience as he ministered.

ZOE SIMPSON

The Support of a Young Colleague

The letter to the Philippians begins with the greeting, "Paul and Timothy, servants of Christ Jesus" (Philippians 1:1). This greeting suggests that Timothy, Paul's protégé, may have assisted him in writing the letter. It is believed that Paul had physical challenges, presumably poor eyesight. It would, therefore, be understandable if he capitalized on Timothy's assistance to write the letter. Whether or not that was the case, the evidence is that, in several ways, Timothy was a significant source of help to Paul throughout his ministry.

According to 2 Timothy 3:15, Timothy came to faith as a young man and was mentored by Paul in the way of the Lord. The relationship between these two men was cemented as they travelled and ministered together. Paul's regard for Timothy as a faithful and dedicated colleague in ministry is evidenced in Philippians 2:19-22:

> I hope in the Lord Jesus to send Timothy to you soon, that I also may be cheered when I receive news about you. I have no one else like him, who will show genuine concern for your welfare. For everyone looks out for their own interests, not those of Jesus Christ. But you know that Timothy has proved himself, because as a son with his father, he has served with me in the work of the Gospel.

The Support of Older Colleagues

In several of his writings, Paul mentioned several older colleagues—both men and women— from whom he derived much support of varying kind, and at various periods of his ministry. However, I wish to draw attention to Epaphroditus as an example of the support that Paul received from his older colleagues during the difficult days of imprisonment.

Writing about Epaphroditus in Philippians 2:25-30, Paul said,

> I think it is necessary to send back to you Epaphroditus, my brother, fellow worker and fellow soldier, who is also your messenger, whom you sent to take care of my needs. … Indeed, he was ill and almost died. But God had mercy on him … I am all the more eager to send him, so that when you see him again you may be glad. … Welcome him in the Lord with great joy, and honour men like him because he almost died for the work of Christ, risking his life to make up for the help you could not give me.

The words "brother", "fellow worker", and "fellow soldier", which Paul used to describe Epaphroditus, are somewhat similar in sentiment to those earlier expressed about Timothy. The words conjure up the picture of someone with whom Paul had a valued and valuable relationship in life and ministry.

Whether young or mature colleagues, there are three equally significant observations made about the relationship Paul had with those who supported him in his ministry. (1) The relationship was established long before the time of Paul's confinement. (2) The relationship transcended the boundaries of age and gender. (3) The relationship was mutually beneficial. In summary, collegial support was circumstantially beneficial to Paul as he navigated challenging days.

The Nature and Extent of Support

Philippians 2:19-24 sheds light on how the support that Paul received from his colleagues helped to meet a variety of needs that he had during the period of his imprisonment

Emotional Support

Although Paul was spiritually mature, the physical separation from his family, friends, and associates may have been emotionally challenging for him. According to 2 Timothy 4:9-11, young Timothy was particularly supportive of Paul during a seemingly emotionally low period when Paul's trusted colleagues had deserted him.

> Do your best to come to me quickly, for Demas, because he loved this world, has deserted me and has gone to Thessalonica. Crescens has gone to Galatia, and Titus to Dalmatia. Only Luke is with me. Get Mark and bring him with you, because he is helpful to me in my ministry.

The expression "do your best to come to me quickly" signals Paul's need for emotional support during the time of his imprisonment. Although he would have been busy praying to God and writing letters to the churches, the prison was a lonely place; the space was not emotionally conducive. Paul was self-aware and mindful of his emotional needs, and he was not abashed to appeal to his support system in this regard.

Welfare Needs

Paul's letter also revealed his need for material supplies. In 2 Timothy 4:13, he asked Timothy to "bring the cloak that I left with Carpus at Troas, and my scrolls, especially the parchments." The winter months were approaching; a cloak would have been needed. Writing helped him to fulfil his ministry and helped him to balance his mental health during the period of confinement. He needed his writing tools.

The believers in Philippi were mindful of Paul's welfare needs and did not wait for him to ask. He was, therefore, blessed with a constant supply of personal care items that the believers sent him through his ministry associates.

Spiritual Support

Due to his confinement, the Apostle Paul was unable to personally visit and encourage the believers. However, they would not be denied spiritual leadership, as he assigned some of his colleagues in ministry to deputize for him.

Paul's colleagues, men and women, the young and the mature, were indispensable to his life and ministry during his difficult experiences. He thought highly of the support he received and seized the opportunities to loudly express his gratitude.

Positioning to Stand Firm

Is there a support group to which you can call during your difficult days? God forbid that you should be devoid of support when you face difficult days. Be proactive in building a support group of individuals who will walk beside you and provide support of various kinds as you navigate difficult days. It will be helpful to know that there is even one person who understands what you are going through; one person who takes the time to be there with and for you.

It is also important for you to position yourself as part of the support system for fellow believers. Make the time to be with them when they need you to be there. Offer a scripture or a word of encouragement in a moment of grief and sorrow. Make a financial contribution if you can; and if you can't, a prayer will always be helpful. The individual whom God lays on your heart is in need of your prayer in the moment; stop and pray as the Holy Spirit leads you to.

In an age when everyone seems to be experiencing difficulties, it becomes challenging for believers to focus on the needs of others. However, the call is for us to be mindful to sometimes prioritize the needs of others over our own. If every believer were to prioritize the needs of another believer, it is highly likely that everyone's needs would be sufficiently met.

However, if you are facing difficult days without needed support from family, friends, or colleagues, rest assured that the Father of compassion and the God of all comfort is ever with you, just like He said He would be, even throughout your difficult days. Ask Him to meet the presenting need, and rest assured that He will.

19.

Support from the Community

Acts 12:1-17

In one of their monthly gatherings, a group of women charted the history of the support group to which they belonged. The recollection included individual testimonies from women who all pointed to the extent of support that they received from the group as they navigated difficult experiences in their individual lives. Toward the close of the session, the women lovingly embraced each other as the song "I Need you to Survive" was quietly played in the background.

Acts 12:1-17 is the passage of focus for the reflections in this chapter. The passage brings to our attention the scenario in which a community of believers applied the principle of support in the circumstances surrounding the Apostle Peter's imprisonment and the threat to his life. An understanding of the context sets the stage for the reflections.

Peter's Experience

The early Church grew exponentially as the Apostles undertook the mandate Jesus gave them to take the message of salvation to Jerusalem, Samaria, and the uttermost parts of the earth (Matthew 28:19). The religious and political leaders of the day stoutly resisted and severely persecuted the Apostles and the adherents of the faith, some to the point of losing their lives.

According to Acts 12:1-4,

> It was about this time that King Herod arrested some who belonged to the church, intending to persecute them. He had James, the brother of John, put to death with the sword. When he saw that this pleased the Jews, he proceeded to seize Peter also. This happened during the Festival of Unleavened Bread. After arresting him, he put him in prison, handing him over to be guarded by four squads of four soldiers each. Herod intended to bring him out for public trial after the Passover.

The Passover was a Jewish festival that commemorated Israel's deliverance from Egypt (Bible Study Tools, n.d., para 2). As the name of the festival suggests, the angel who was assigned to kill the firstborn in every Egyptian house passed over the house of the Israelites at the sight of the blood that they were instructed to daub over the doorpost of their houses. How ironic, then, that the king and his adherents could so quickly transition from celebrating life to celebrating death. Such is the callousness of the hearts of persons in power who avail themselves to be used by the enemy of the faith.

Although Peter's trial was delayed until after the end of the Passover festival, his fate was already sealed! He would be put to death by the king's unalterable order. This reality had a deleterious effect on the body of believers. The believers' response to Peter's predicament is one of the primary points for consideration in this chapter.

The Response of the Body of Believers

The response of the body of believers to Peter's predicament is highlighted in Acts 12:5: "So Peter was kept in prison, but the church was earnestly praying to God for him." The believers could have appealed to the king for Peter's release, but they chose, instead, to appeal to God through prayer. They could have taken cover for their own lives. Instead, they resorted to prayer. It is quite clear that the believers knew that praying is what the church does when there is trouble. There are, therefore, three observations made regarding this prayerful response of the body of believers.

The Immediacy of the Response

The first observation is the immediacy of the response. The indication is that the believers knew what to do in the face of challenges of this nature. They knew to whom they should turn for help in these situations. They were about the business of the Lord, and they immediately turned to Him in prayer for help in this challenging situation.

The Display of Solidarity

The second observation is the solidarity that prevailed among the believers in the face of Peter's imprisonment and the threat of death. The indication is that they were in the situation together. Peter may have been alone inside the prison, but outside was a force that stood in solidarity with him. The believers were not blood-related, at least not biologically. They were spiritually related by the blood of Christ Jesus, the One for whom they were collectively being persecuted.

To prayerfully stand in solidarity with Peter signalled that the believers were not focused on their own interests. If that were the case, they could have prayed for themselves in the confines of their homes and the privacy of their hearts. But that was not the case. The sense here is that they gathered as a unified body in prayerful support of the brother.

The Intensity of Their Praying

According to Acts 12:5, "... the church was earnestly praying to God for him [Peter]." This was a matter of life and death. The king was bent on pleasing the crowd and on pleasing himself. As soon as the Passover celebrations ended, Peter would have been killed. This matter at hand required more than a make-mention-of-him prayer; it required deep intercession on Peter's behalf. Of course, no prayer is ordinary, but some situations require a greater depth and intensity of prayer than others.

The passage does not indicate the specific matters about which the believers were praying. However, it can well be imagined that prayers were offered for Peter's release from prison, and for the sentence of death to be annulled. There was also room for the prayers to include petitions for the believers to be emboldened with courage to face opposition and to hold fast to the faith amidst persecution.

The believers may also have prayed for the continued growth of the fledgling church despite the intensity of the prevailing persecution. The reality of the day was that Peter was in prison and would have been killed in short order. There was nothing that the believers could have done to change the king's edict, but they certainly could bring that difficult situation to the Sovereign God, and they did.

The Result that Prayers Bring

In response to the believers' prayers, God did the miraculous, as recorded in Acts 12:7-9.

> Suddenly, an angel of the Lord appeared and a light shone in the cell. He struck Peter on the side and woke him up. "Quick, get up!" he said, and the chains fell off Peter's wrists. Then the angel said to him, "Put on your clothes and sandals." And Peter did so. "Wrap your cloak around you and follow me," the angel told him. Peter followed him out of the prison, but he had no idea that what the angel was really happening; he thought he was seeing a vision.

The fact that the angel had to smite Peter to awaken him suggests that he was in a very deep sleep. Sleep may have mentally removed him from the reality of his impending death. He may have resigned himself to the circumstances over which he had no control. He may have been at peace with the situation, confident that the body of believers would have been praying for him.

Regardless of the conjecture, the reality is that while the community of believers earnestly prayed for Peter, the angel of God visited him in his cell. The angel then instructed Peter to get dressed and follow him out through the iron gates, in the presence of the prison guards, into freedom. The earnest prayers of the believers were answered in an extraordinary way.

Positioning to Stand Firm

The support that the community of believers offers its members cannot be overstated and should not be underestimated. Collective prayer should become the order of the day in the Christian community, especially during difficult days.

Among my own lived experiences of difficult days is one in which I suffered a prolonged period of ill health and confinement. I was en route to a church to make a Sunday morning presentation when I sustained injury to my back as a gate with an estimated weight of 500 lbs. (227 kg.) dislodged its track and fell on me.

The fractured bones in my lower back necessitated hospitalization, and seven weeks of lying in one position with traction on one of my legs. I resigned myself to the reality of a steady dose of painkillers, daily injections to prevent blood clotting, and having my personal care needs met by others. Admittedly, I was frightened by the thought that I would be unable to move in the event of an emergency and the possibility of long-term deformity.

During those difficult days of intense pain and discomfiting confinement, the medical team provided expert intervention to ensure physical recovery. Notwithstanding, I was kept from emotional and spiritual collapse by the psycho-social and prayerful support of the members of my immediate family, my circle of friends, and the church community.

I well remember the sister who repeatedly sent me a supply of bottled water and reminded me to keep hydrated. On my discharge from the hospital, a nurse from the church community administered the daily anti-clotting injections, and another, although she lives overseas, called almost daily to check on me. Another sister offered financial support that equated to my salary when the period of recovery exhausted the allotted paid leave of absence. Countless brothers and sisters, as well as groups of believers, prayed with me in person or remotely. Such is the practical support of the body of believers in challenging times.

The call of the reflections in this chapter is for believers within the Christian community to stand in solidarity with those who are persecuted, afflicted, burdened by their realities, and challenged in one form or another. We hear of brothers and sisters in countries where they are persecuted for the name of Christ. How do other believers respond? Support may take various forms, such as monetary gifts, a word of encouragement, or physical presence. In whatever way possible, the body of believers should endeavour to support those who are faced with challenging circumstances.

If there is nothing else that believers can do for each other, they can offer their prayerful support. Pray for God's intervention in the matter. Pray for divine protection and courage to stand firm in the faith. Pray for increased resources. Pray individually and collectively. Expend the time and effort to pray in support of other believers.

The outcome of prayers may not always be the expected. The outcome is entirely up to God's intent and desires. The duty of every believer is to pray and trust God for His will to be done on earth as it is in heaven.

20.

When Difficult Days End

Job 42:7-17

I n her book "Better Than I Dreamed", C. Ruth Taylor
shares snippets of her lived experiences that had
outcomes that surpassed her initial expectations.

The book of Job ends with a "Better Than I Dreamed"
account of the life of the main character. Two previous
chapters examined how Job kept his faith in God during his
difficult days of adversity and loneliness. Throughout his
ordeal, Job desperately cried to God for intervention and
relief.

God eventually responded to Job's cries in a lengthy
discourse, in which He drew Job's attention to His might and
majesty (Job 38-41). Job was humbled and silenced by God's
response. The only words Job had were words of repentance
and confession. Whereas he had heard about God prior to

his trials, he had only then come to experientially know God (Job 42:1-6).

Job's experience again comes into focus in this chapter, which examines his circumstances at the end of his difficult days. Job 42:7-17 is the scripture of focus from which two observations will be highlighted: God's evaluation of Job and his friends, and God's restoration of all that Job had lost.

God's Evaluation

Following Job's repentance, God continued to speak, first to Job's friends and then to Job himself. An examination of God's words in this context reveals that they were nothing short of an evaluation of how Job and his friends postured during the challenging period. God's evaluation of Job's friends is reflected in the words of condemnation that He had for them.

Words of Condemnation

Job 42:7-8 reveals the basis for God's displeasure with Job's friends.

After the Lord had said these things to Job, he said to Eliphaz the Temanite, I am angry with you and your two friends, because you have not spoken of me what is right, as my servant Job has. So now take seven bulls and seven rams and go to my servant Job and sacrifice a burnt offering for yourselves. My servant Job will pray for you, and I will accept his prayer and not deal with you according to your folly.

The charge that God had against Job's friends was grounded in what they said about Him during their conversations with Job as he experienced difficult days. Although the men had much to say about God, their utterances did not reflect a correct knowledge and understanding of God's character.

The Matthew Henry Concise Bible Commentary explains that "Job's friends had wronged God, by making prosperity a mark of the true church, and affliction a certain proof of God's wrath" (Bible Hub). This was not a true representation of God. Therefore, God condemned the men's utterances and instructed them to repent. The men were required to offer a burnt sacrifice—an offering for sin, and to go to Job, who would then say a prayer for them.

Words of Commendation

God had words of commendation for Job, much in contrast to the words of condemnation that He had for Job's friends. In God's assessment of Job's utterances during his difficult days, He concluded that Job uttered the "right words" about Him, and by extension, the right words about His character. Matthew Henry observed that "Job had referred things to the future judgment and the future state, more than his friends …" (Bible Hub). Job 1:22 summarizes the "right words" and the right posture of Job's heart toward God: "In all this, Job did not sin by charging God with wrongdoing."

Job's "right words" about God qualified him to intercede for his friends. Since Job had the right words about God, he would likewise have the right words to say to God on behalf of his friends. He could ask God to be merciful to the men because he knew God to be a merciful God. God would listen to Job as he interceded for the men using the right words about God, and the right words to God.

The commendation that God had for Job is reflected in the title "servant" that God accorded to Job. As the Devil sought permission to afflict Job, God referred to him as being his servant (Job 1:8). As God spoke to Job's friends at the end of Job's trials, God again referred to Job as His servant three times in as many sentences: "… you have not spoken of me what is right, as my servant Job has." "… go to my servant Job …", "My servant Job will pray for you" (Job 42:7-8).

The indication is that God was pleased with this man, Job, who had walked in integrity both in prosperity and in adversity. The posture that Job assumed during his difficult days exemplified the qualities that easily identified and distinguished him as a servant of God: integrity, purity, and humility.

Despite his experience of adversity, there was no trace of bitterness or unforgiveness in Job's heart for his countrymen who had mistreated him, or his friends who had misrepresented him. There was no trace of resentment in his heart toward his wife, who had given him unsound advice instead of continued support. God could, therefore, have readily depended on His servant Job to intercede for his friends. God had no issue attending to the prayers of the man who was His servant at heart.

The Restoration

The second observation is the restoration that became Job's reality at the end of his difficult experience. According to Job 42:10, "After Job had prayed for his friends, the Lord made him prosperous again and gave him twice as much as he had before." There may be significance in the fact that it was after

Job prayed for his friends that the Lord blessed him. However, it is the restoration itself to which we give primacy.

Job 42:12-15 describes the extent of the restoration Job enjoyed:

> The Lord blessed the latter part of Job's life more than the first. He had fourteen thousand sheep, six thousand camels, a thousand yoke of oxen and a thousand donkeys. And he also had seven sons and three daughters. ... Nowhere in all the land were there found women as beautiful as Job's daughters, ...

The posture that Job assumed during the difficult experience of adversity disproved Satan's hypothesis that there is a direct correlation between faith and blessings. The incontrovertible evidence was that Job's faith in God was not premised on material possessions. Therefore, God had no issue blessing Job again, and this time with much more than he previously had.

Although nothing is said about Job's wife at the point of restoration, she, too, enjoyed the restoration that Job enjoyed. She would have grieved the loss of her children during the period of Job's adversity, but now she enjoyed the blessing of having ten children.

Job 42:16-17 is a fitting summary of Job's life and experience. "After this, Job lived a hundred and forty years; he saw his children and their children to the fourth generation. And so he died, old and full of years." It does not get better than that!

Positioning to Stand Firm

Difficult days do not last forever. The question is, what evaluation will we receive from God about our posture and practice during our difficult days? We do well to begin by doing our own self-evaluation. What have we been saying about God during your difficult days? What we say reflects our thoughts and the condition of our hearts. As a fact, the condition of our hearts will be shaped by our knowledge of God.

In the depths of his difficult days, Job had the "right words" to say about God because of what he knew about God. Job particularly knew and was confident that God is faithful and He fulfils his promises. Hear again Job's "right words": "I know that my Redeemer lives, and that in the end he will stand on the earth. And after my skin has been destroyed, yet in my flesh I will see God; I myself will see him" (Job 19:25-27).

We do well to clarify our perceptions of God and, therefore, position ourselves to have the "right words" of praise and adoration for God, even during our difficult days. We should also be mindful of the words we use in conversations about others, especially those who are unkind to us. People may mistreat us, misrepresent us, or forsake us. The temptation is to say unkind things about the individuals, but that is not for us to do.

Matthew 5:11 is most applicable in these difficult situations: "Blessed are you when people insult you, persecute you and falsely say all kinds of evil against you because of me [Jesus]." In these challenging situations, the believer is encouraged to "rejoice and be glad, because great is your reward in heaven, for in the same way they persecuted the prophets who were before you" (Matthew 5:12).

There is much to be said about forgiving others who are unkind to us. Forgiveness keeps us emotionally whole and spiritually strong. Forgiveness places us in good standing with God and frees us to live the abundant life. Let us make it a practice to forgive those who have unfairly and unkindly treated us. Let us determine to pray for them and let them go!

There is a sense in which we would better endure our difficult days were we to see the end at the beginning. However, we cannot necessarily tell how our respective experiences will end. We do not know whether anything will change soon or if it will change at all; we simply do not know!

However, since we do know the God who knows all things, we can put our questions about the future to rest.

Since we know the God of peace, we can trust Him to give us peace during our storms. Since we know that God is the source and the strength of our lives, and He promised to keep us from falling and to present us faultless to His Father (Jude 1:24), we can triumph in our difficult days and live to the praise of the most holy name of Christ Jesus.

Conclusion

Teacher Pat, as I affectionately call her, concluded her testimony of victory that she shared with me with the words: "If you do not have a battle, you can never shout for victory." As her story goes, she had been battling a bout of physical complications from a medical condition for several months. There were days when she felt that she was at the point of death and was only returned to life by the Holy Spirit. I reference Teacher Pat's experience and testimony (with her permission) as a fitting conclusion to the scriptural reflections in this book.

Believers of past ages experienced difficult days that tested their faith and resolve beyond measure. Their experiences reflect a range of human experiences and, more so, the shades of persecution that had become the order of the times in which they lived. Since difficult days are the common experience of Christ followers, believers in this present age will similarly experience difficult days that could eventually be of unparalleled magnitude.

Regardless of the nature of the experiences, our faith will be severely tested. In these circumstances, those who know God, know what He said, and are firmly grounded in their faith, will remain standing throughout the difficult experiences. The question, therefore, is how prepared are we to face our difficult days? What posture will we assume when we are called to take the stand for Christ? Will we resolutely stand firm in the faith during our difficult days?

The lives of believers from past ages serve as models for those of this present age and the future. Since the believers of the past persevered and prevailed during their difficult days, so too can believers of the present age and the age to come. Hebrews 12:1-3 call attention to the example of believers of past ages and offer encouragement for believers today:

> Therefore, since we are surrounded by such a great cloud of witnesses, let us throw off everything that hinders and the sin that so easily entangles. And let us run with perseverance the race marked out for us. Let us fix our eyes on Jesus, the author and perfector of our faith, who for the joy set before him endured the cross, scorning its shame, and sat down at the right hand of the throne of God. Consider him who endured

such opposition from sinful men, so that you
will not grow weary and lose heart.

Believers do well to remember that trials do not last
forever. Jesus promised to return and take His children to be
with Him (John 14:3). Until then, we commit to support each
other and to rely on the Holy Spirit to help us remain
steadfast in our faith until the difficult days pass and give way
to a glorious end.

Acknowledgements

My friend, Grace Shields Powell, has repeatedly encouraged me to publish these scriptural reflections for the benefit of a wider audience. However, I have long hesitated to do so, on account of a sense of inadequacy. Her constant encouragement has now borne fruit.

Except for Chapter 5, the scriptural reflections in this book were delivered on the "Grace Hour" radio programme when I served as the Director of Christian Education of the Missionary Church in Jamaica (MCAJ). I acknowledge, with gratitude, the moral and editorial support that Reverend Rennard White and Revered Dr. Sam Green, under whose presidency I served, provided as I journeyed through the writing process. The critical editorial reviews given by Dr. Hadyn Marshall, Reverend Patricia Salmon, and Dr. Amoy Rhoe are also acknowledged with gratitude.

This project was completed under the expert guidance of C. Ruth Taylor, the founder of Authorpreneur Secrets Academy. I would have long discontinued the project had it not been for her constant encouragement.

My husband, Reverend Stephen Luke Simpson, and my sons, John-Mark and Jonathan, journeyed with me through my lived experiences of difficult days. Their support has given me the impetus to encourage others to stand firm in their faith during difficult times.

References

American Psychological Association. (n.d.), Anxiety. https://www.apa.org/topics/anxiety

Chase, M. (2024, June). Through the Valley: 8 Lessons from Job about Suffering & Comfort. https://www.logos.com/grow/nook-job-and-suffering/

Christianity, Nov. 10, 2015. https://christianity.stackexchange.com/questions/14163/is-there-a-difference-between-prayer-and-petition#:~:text=As%20such%20one%20could%20parse%20the%20verse,would%20be%20how%20the%20prayer%20is%20done.

Christianity.com. (n.d.). Matthew Henry Commentary Complete. https://www.christianity.com/bible/commentary/matthew-henry-complete/philippians/4

Folkes, L. (1970). Philippians. In D. Guthrie, and J. A. Motyer, (Eds.), *The New Bible Commentary Revised* (pp. 1125-1138). Intervarsity-Press.

Global Disciples Canada (October 30, 2023). https://www.globaldisciples.ca/blog/the-joy-of-the-lord-is-my-strength-serving-each-other-with-joy/#:~:text=However%2C%20the%20joy%20found%20in,source%20of%20resilience%20and%20endurance.

Heavenor, E. S. P. (1970). Job. In D. Guthrie, and J. A. Motyer, (Eds.), *The New Bible Commentary Revised* (pp. 421-445). Intervarsity-Press.

Henry, M. (N.D.), Bible Study Tools, https://www.biblestudytools.com/commentaries/matthew-henry-concise/exodus/12.html

Holy Bible, 1987, International Bible Society New International Version.

Matthew Henry's Bible Commentary Christianity.comhttps://www.christianity.com/bible/commentary/matthew-henry-complete/job/1

Matthew Henry's Commentary: Philippians 4. (n.d.) https://biblehub.com/commentaries/mhc/philippians/4.htm

Matthew Henry's Bible Commentary. Christianity.com, https://www.christianity.com/bible/commentary/matthew-henry-concise/philippians/1

Matthew Henry's Concise Commentary (n.d.). Job 42:7, Bible Hub.com, https://biblehub.com/commentaries/job/42-7.htm

Murthy, V. H. (2023). Our Epidemic of Loneliness and Isolation: The U.S. Surgeon General's Advisory on the Healing Effects of Social Connection and Community. https://www.hhs.gov/sites/default/files/surgeon-general-social-connection-advisory.pdf

Piper, J. (April 29, 2016), Desiring God, https://www.desiringgod.org/interviews/what-is-worship

Marshall, L. H. (1970). Luke. In D. Guthrie, and J. A. Motyer, (Eds.), *The New Bible Commentary Revised* (pp. 887-925). Intervarsity-Press.

Schoenberg, S. (n.d.). Jewish Virtual Library.
https://www.jewishvirtuallibrary.org/the-sanhedrin

Wylie, S. (June 26, 2023), Courage,
https://www.wisdomonline.org/blog/courage/#:~:text
=The%20biblical%20characteristic%20of%20courage,o
n%20His%20strength%20and%20guidance

Made in the USA
Middletown, DE
20 October 2025

19359405R00113